Library Website Design and Development

Library Website Design and Development
Trends and Best Practices

Brighid M. Gonzales

ROWMAN & LITTLEFIELD
Lanham • Boulder • New York • London

Published by Rowman & Littlefield
An imprint of The Rowman & Littlefield Publishing Group, Inc.
4501 Forbes Boulevard, Suite 200, Lanham, Maryland 20706
www.rowman.com

86-90 Paul Street, London EC2A 4NE

Copyright © 2025 by The Rowman & Littlefield Publishing Group, Inc.

All rights reserved. No part of this book may be reproduced in any form or by any electronic or mechanical means, including information storage and retrieval systems, without written permission from the publisher, except by a reviewer who may quote passages in a review.

British Library Cataloguing in Publication Information Available

Library of Congress Cataloging-in-Publication Data Available

ISBN 978-1-5381-9234-4 (cloth: alk. paper)
ISBN 978-1-5381-9235-1 (pbk.: alk. paper)
ISBN 978-1-5381-9236-8 (electronic)

∞™ The paper used in this publication meets the minimum requirements of American National Standard for Information Sciences—Permanence of Paper for Printed Library Materials, ANSI/NISO Z39.48-1992.

Contents

Preface		vii
Chapter 1:	Website Design Standards and Best Practices	1
Chapter 2:	Trends in Library Website Design	21
Chapter 3:	Content Management Systems	35
Chapter 4:	Content Strategy: Inventories, Audits, and Needs Assessment	49
Chapter 5:	Information Architecture and Navigation Design	63
Chapter 6:	User Experience Design and Usability Testing	77
Chapter 7:	Accessibility and Universal Design	93
Chapter 8:	Website Security and Data Privacy	111
Chapter 9:	Assessment and Analytics	127
Chapter 10:	Ongoing Maintenance	141
Index		153
About the Author		159

Preface

While there have been many books written about website design and development from a general industry standpoint, there are relatively few books focused on the distinct needs and concerns of library websites. The published titles on library websites are often books that take a deep dive into a specific subject area of library website design, such as privacy,[1] accessibility,[2] or writing for the web.[3] In publishing this book, I hope to provide an inclusive guide to all the topics and steps inherent in the process of website design and development, while also providing a focused guide on the unique needs of library websites. Each chapter in this book covers the foundational knowledge needed for an aspect of website design and is supplemented by a list of additional resources that go into further depth on each topic.

The book starts with basic design concepts and covers the best practices, conventions, and standards of general website design, along with guidelines for writing, choosing typefaces and colors, and creating a style guide. The first chapter also includes fifteen current trends in website design that library website designers should be aware of, while chapter 2 goes into specifics regarding trends in website design for libraries. This includes best practices and popular features found on both academic and public library websites. Chapter 2 also showcases some examples of exceptional website designs from academic, public, and state libraries.

Chapter 3 goes into some of the technical aspects of website development—namely, choosing a content management system. This chapter discusses various CMS architectures and what to consider when evaluating a potential CMS. A comparison of popular content management systems and a rundown of some of the systems designed specifically for libraries is also included.

Chapters 4 through 8 go into detail about the individual aspects of the website design process, including content strategy, information architecture, navigation design, usability, accessibility, security, and privacy. Each chapter provides background information about the topic, guidelines on how to perform explicit processes, and recommendations for using the data gathered to inform the design process. Some of the processes covered in this section include:

- How to conduct a content inventory and a content audit
- How to conduct a needs assessment
- How to gather user feedback and use it develop your website structure
- How to determine the labels for your menu items
- How to conduct user research and usability testing
- How to meet WCAG guidelines for accessibility
- How to evaluate your website for accessibility compliance
- How to protect your website from security threats and attacks
- How to evaluate the security of your website
- How to conduct a privacy audit
- How to write a data privacy policy

The end of the book details what should happen after the new website has been launched, from assessing and recommending incremental design improvements that will keep your new website fresh and user-friendly, to analyzing website performance data to make data-driven design decisions. The final chapter outlines how to maintain the website going forward, including important maintenance tasks, developing a website governance plan, and creating an ongoing maintenance schedule.

Designing or redesigning a new website can be a major undertaking and can seem especially overwhelming for small libraries with limited staff or in-house expertise. My hope for this book is that it will serve as a guide for libraries and librarians facing a website design or redesign project and will lead them through each step of the design process, providing the foundational information, best practices, and resources to help them successfully design and launch their new website.

NOTES

1. Marshall Breeding, "Protecting Privacy on Library Websites: Critical Technologies and Implementation Trends," *Library Technology Reports* 55, no. 7 (2019), https://doi.org/10.5860/ltr.55n7.
2. Laura Francabandera, *Making Library Websites Accessible: A Practical Guide for Librarians* (Lanham: Rowman & Littlefield, 2018).
3. Rebecca Blakiston, *Writing Effectively in Print and on the Web: A Practical Guide for Librarians* (Lanham: Rowman & Littlefield, 2017).

BIBLIOGRAPHY

Blakiston, Rebecca. *Writing Effectively in Print and on the Web: A Practical Guide for Librarians.* Lanham: Rowman & Littlefield, 2017.

Breeding, Marshall. "Protecting Privacy on Library Websites: Critical Technologies and Implementation Trends." *Library Technology Reports* 55, no. 7 (2019). https://doi.org/10.5860/ltr.55n7.

Francabandera, Laura. *Making Library Websites Accessible: A Practical Guide for Librarians.* Lanham: Rowman & Littlefield, 2018.

1
Website Design Standards and Best Practices

Designing a new library website might seem like an overwhelming project at first, but there is a vast amount of information written about general website design that can help you move through the process more easily. Whether redesigning an existing website or creating a brand-new website design, you also don't need to start completely from scratch. The field of web design has a number of widely accepted best practices and conventions that can guide you as you plan your new site. While these have evolved since the beginning of the web, many of the best practices have remained relatively consistent, or have been refined, throughout the years. By following these guidelines and best practices, you can ensure that your website has a positive "impact on users' perception of the professionalism of your site and of your library."[1]

While designing a library website may have some differences from designing an e-commerce or promotional website, the basic design rules for what makes a website look good will still apply. In fact, these best practices should form the basis of your design before you think about the customizations it may require specifically for library users.

A website design that is considered visually aesthetically pleasing will "use consistent typography, establish a clear hierarchy, utilize a refined color palette, and align to a grid."[2] These rules of visual design are what make a website look "good" and "professional," as opposed to disorganized, amateur, or even untrustworthy.

Some of the common elements of good website design include:

- Grid system: using a grid helps align text and other elements on the site and maintain consistency of the site's layout across all pages.
- Refined color palette: Limiting your color selection to just a few different colors that are complementary will make the overall color palette look more refined.

- Clear visual hierarchy: Aligning the elements on your site with a clear visual hierarchy will draw the viewer's eye to the most important content first.
- High-quality images: Using high-quality images that add to the design rather than being purely decorative enhances the visual quality of the site.
- Use of space: Including enough white space will make your site more readable to users and keep it from seeming cluttered.
- Consistency: Consistency in font, spacing, color, and other design elements is what gives your website a professional look. Carefully choose your design styles and maintain those throughout the entire website.

Some designers like to base their designs on what's known as the golden ratio: "Two quantities a and b (a>b) are in the golden ratio φ if their ratio is the same as the ratio of their sum to the larger of the two quantities."[3] This system of proportionality gives balance to a design and makes it aesthetically pleasing. The golden ratio may seem aesthetically pleasing to humans because it can be found in many patterns in nature, for example, seashells, galaxies, and hurricanes.

The golden ratio can be implemented in a rectangular or a spiral design pattern. Using the golden rectangle provides a visually aesthetic way of dividing the layout into a grid pattern, naturally creating a sidebar and a main content area. These areas can also be further divided using the same ratio. The golden spiral can be used to create a strong composition when cropping images, by locating the spiral over the main focus of the image.

Text can also be designed with the golden ratio by using the proportions to determine the size of the font for a heading compared to body text, as well as for defining line height. While the golden ratio can be a good way to structure and balance a design, it can be difficult to maintain in a responsive website that adjusts to screen size.

Much research has been done in the field of website design and usability about the way most people use the internet. Some of the truths that have been discovered are that:

- Users don't read text: Users scan text rather than reading through every word, so the ability to scan through the text on your site, through the use of headings and bullet points, is a must.
- Users are impatient: If users cannot figure out how to use your site within a few seconds, they will leave. Navigation must be intuitive.
- Users don't make good choices: Most users employ a concept known as *satisficing*, or choosing the first decent-looking option rather than searching for the best option. Make choosing the best option easy for them.
- Users will muddle through: Most users won't read directions. They won't take the time to learn how things work. They'll just muddle through the

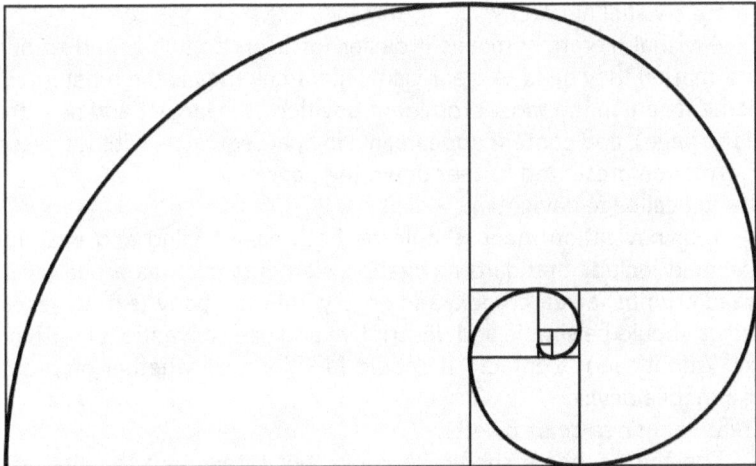

Figure 1.1 The Golden Ratio. https://openclipart.org/detail/339085/fibonacci-spiral.

best that they can. Again, make it easy, make it intuitive, and don't make the user think.
- Users want control: Users want to control the browser and their own online experience. Don't take that control away from them.[4] Let them choose whenever possible.

WEBSITE DESIGN BEST PRACTICES

The field of website design relies on several best practices that should be kept in mind when designing a new site. Although sometimes design rules can be broken to great effect, it is vital to understand the rules that will give your site a polished, professional look before deciding if and when to deviate. Here are twenty generally-agreed-upon best practices, some of which come directly from the principles of aesthetic design described above.

1. Follow user-centered design practices.
    The website should be designed with the users' wants and needs considered up front. The identity of your users and their specific needs should inform your design choices, including fonts, colors, and navigation.
2. Use a grid or follow common design patterns.
    Grid layouts make the website look neat and organized and help keep elements like text and images aligned. Eye-tracking studies have shown that website visitors scan information in an F-shaped pattern, reading the top of the page first, down the left side, and then across. This pattern can help you determine where to position important elements on the site.

3. Create a visual hierarchy.

    A visual hierarchy makes it easier for users to follow and to find the information they need. A clear visual hierarchy means the most important elements are in the most prominent position (the largest and near the top of the page), and content appears in a logical sequence, with less essential information presented further down the page.

4. Use logical page navigation.

    Your navigation menu should be both easy to find and easy to use. It should include standard navigation elements such as a header menu, bread crumbs, a search box, and links within the body text as necessary. Labels should be simple and descriptive and use conventional terminology like "About" and "Contact." It should function well whether on a desktop or a mobile device.

5. Create a refined color palette.

    The color scheme should be consistent throughout the site, and the colors chosen should complement each other. Colors should be either next to each other, or opposite each other on the color wheel. You should also avoid using too many different colors. Two to five colors is considered optimal for aesthetic design.

6. Use high-quality, web-optimized images.

    The images you choose should be of high quality and high resolution, and they should contribute to the overall design. Compressed images will load more quickly on the page, improving page speed. Images should also be responsive across different-sized devices and should include alt-text for accessibility.

7. Use buttons and links correctly.

    Buttons should look like buttons and stand out from the rest of the elements on the site. Likewise, links should be easily recognizable as links, by being underlined and/or in a different color from the rest of the text. Regular text should never be underlined or made a different color, as users may confuse it for a link.

8. Make text readable.

    Text should be readable no matter what size (consider users who need to zoom in on text to read it) and whether it's being read on a desktop or mobile device. Some fonts that are considered "web-friendly" include Times New Roman, Helvetica, Arial, Veranda, and Courier New. Generally, no more than three typefaces in three sizes should be used. Text should also be broken up into small chunks rather than presented in large text blocks, as these can be difficult to read and can make the site look cluttered. Headings and bullet points also help to make the site more scannable. Text color should have adequate contrast with the background color for clear visibility.

9. Leave enough space.

    You don't want your site to look cluttered or crowded. This can make it difficult for users to read or to find the information they need. Negative spacing can help draw attention to the most important content and make text easier to read. Spacing can also be used to group related content together visually.

10. Keep things simple.

    A simple page design will look uncluttered, will seem more professional, and will keep down page load times. This means using a limited color palette, a limited number of typefaces and font sizes, and a judicious use of graphics. Simplicity will also make the site more accessible and easier to make responsive.

11. Keep things consistent.

    Consistency is what makes your website look professional and lends credibility to your organization. Inconsistency can lead the visitor to distrust your site and the information they find there. This means all elements, like fonts, icons, colors, spacing, and layout, should be used consistently across the entire website.

12. Make it responsive.

    Your website should look visually appealing and be completely functional no matter what size device the visitor is using. This means that images should scale up or down according to screen size, and navigation, headings, and text should realign themselves as the screen size is reduced. A grid layout or framework (such as Bootstrap) can help with this.

13. Make it accessible.

    Accessibility is important so that all visitors can easily make use of your site. It is also often a legal requirement that websites be accessible. An accessible website uses alt-text for images, can be navigated without a mouse, and has adequate color contrast, among other guidelines.

14. Make it fast.

    A slow-loading website can deter visitors and cause them to leave the site before they are able to find what they need. You can ensure that your page loads quickly by minimizing the use of large files and plugins, and not including any unnecessary code.

15. Make it secure.

    Secure the site against cyberattacks by using a secure web host, firewalls, encryption, SSL certification, and anti-virus and anti-malware software. Limit login attempts to prevent unauthorized access. Mandate the use of strong passwords and use two-factor authentication. If your site is hacked, it can be vandalized, or you can lose access to it altogether. Your users' personal information may also be at risk, and a security breach can decrease trust in your website and organization.

16. Think about SEO.

    There are many things you can do to optimize SEO (search engine optimization), including ensuring your website loads quickly, uses strategic keywords, and is mobile-friendly. Using proper headings and subheadings, alt-text on images, and clear URLs also enhances SEO. SEO optimization increases the visibility of your site and makes it easier for users to find.

17. Connect social media.

    Use recognizable social media icons to link users to your social media accounts. You can also make content sharable through social media so that users can share content to their own networks.

18. Personalize the site for the user.

    Making the site personalized for each user provides a better user experience. This can include allowing the user to personalize the layout on their account page, utilizing targeted content, or providing recommendations based on their previous history. You can also create specialized content or pathways based on audience segments to offer more personalization.

19. Continuously improve your design.

    Even if your design seems perfect at first, chances are good that it can be improved. User testing can help you identify areas for improvement or discover missing or hard-to-find elements. Design trends also change over time, and an iterative design process can keep your site looking fresh and modern without the need for a complete design overhaul.

20. Follow standard website conventions.

    Website conventions are conventions because they are widely used. Users have seen hundreds of websites and have come to expect these conventions. Not using web conventions causes confusion and increased difficulty for your users.

CONVENTIONS AND STANDARDS

Website conventions should always be used so that visitors feel comfortable and familiar with your site and aren't confused by unexpected elements. Usability expert Jakob Nielsen defines a *standard* as an element that is used in 80 percent or more of all websites. A *convention* is an element that is also used frequently enough that visitors will expect it (they will recognize it from between 50 and 80 percent of other websites they have visited). Elements used by less than half of existing sites (or elements that are unconventional or non-standard) should be avoided, as they simply confuse users.[5]

Nielsen advises that the use of standards ensures that your website visitors know what to expect, know how to find and use common features, and experience greater overall satisfaction with your website. Table 1.1 includes website conventions and standards that your visitors will expect to see when they arrive at your site.

DESIGN MISTAKES TO AVOID

If you follow the website design best practices listed above, it's unlikely you'll make the mistakes listed below. However, it's good to be aware of them and make sure that your site doesn't suffer from these potential design flaws:

- Large walls of text: Most users won't read long paragraphs of text. Break it up, use headings, incorporate bullet points, and keep paragraphs short.
- Overcrowded layout: An overcrowded layout can lead to cognitive overload and overwhelm the user. Websites are easier to use when they maintain a simple design and include plenty of white space.
- Complex navigation: Navigation should be easy, intuitive, and prominent. If the user can't find what they need right away, they will leave.
- Poor readability: Poor readability can be caused by text that is too close together or set in hard-to-read fonts or a low color contrast.

Table 1.1 Conventional usage of common website elements.

Element	Conventional Usage
Logo	A website logo should appear in the top left or top center of the page and should link the user back to the homepage no matter where they are on the site.
Navigation	The main navigation should appear at the top of the website. Secondary navigation should be on the left side of the page or near the top. It should look clickable and use common navigation patterns such as the hamburger menu, dropdown, or tabs. A hamburger icon should mean that the menu is expandable.
Icons	Icons should be recognizable from their widespread use on other apps and websites. For example, the gear icon represents settings, the envelope icon represents email, and the shopping cart icon represents checkout. Social media links should also use their designated brand icons.
Buttons and Links	Links should be underlined or use a different color of text. Buttons should look clearly clickable, be shaped like a button, and use a 3D effect. Links and buttons should change color when hovered over with a mouse.
Search bar	A search bar, if included, should appear in the top right or top center of the page. If a website is very large, users will expect to see a search bar.
Text	Text should not be underlined or appear in a different color if it's not a link. Red text should indicate an error message.
Layout	The layout of the site should be consistent with that of other websites within the industry.

- Media autoplay: Many users will be annoyed by media files that play automatically when the page loads. It also takes control away from the user. Let them choose when or if to play audio and video content.
- Not mobile-friendly: Over half of all web traffic now comes from mobile devices.[6] If your website is unusable on a mobile device, many users won't use it at all.
- Poor accessibility: Accessibility for all users is important and, in many cases, legally required. Test thoroughly to ensure your site is accessible to everyone.
- Pop-ups: Pop-ups are another thing that will annoy your users, and many will have pop-up blocking software installed in their browser to prevent them. The use of pop-ups can also make your site seem untrustworthy.
- Lack of contact information or an "About Us" page: Another sign of an untrustworthy website is a lack of contact information or lack of information about the organization. Include multiple contact methods, such as phone and email, which also helps with accessibility.
- Lack of SSL certification: All websites today should have an SSL certificate installed to verify their identity, especially if you are selling anything or collecting personal data. Most users won't trust a site without one, and browsers will warn visitors that the site may be dangerous.
- Slow loading times: We know website users are impatient. If your site is slow to load, many will give up and go elsewhere.
- Inconsistency: Inconsistency across your website makes it look less professional and your organization seem less trustworthy.

STYLE GUIDELINES

When deciding on what styles to use for your website, some important areas to focus on are the writing, typography, and color palette. These elements can make a big difference to the look and feel of your site, how professional and trustworthy it seems, and the site's overall usability. This section discusses some of the best practices for writing on the web, choosing typography, and deciding on a color palette.

Writing for the Web

At first glance, it might seem that writing content for the web is no different from writing any other content, but this is untrue. Newspapers, magazines, and even books can contain pages of paragraph after paragraph, and readers will read through the whole thing. That's because when they pick up a newspaper or a book, they are there to read a story. But users don't come to your website to read a story; they come to find information or complete a task. And no matter how much text you cull from a first draft or how much you refine the writing, they still won't read everything on the page. In fact, Jakob Nielsen found that on average, website visitors only read about 18 percent of words on a webpage, and as the number of words increases, the percentage they read goes down.[7]

That is what makes writing for the web difficult. You know that users won't read everything, so you have to make sure that what they do read is the information they actually need. There are several rules for writing for the web that can help you write content so that your users will be able to quickly and easily find what they need.

1. Identify your audience: Who are they, and what do they need to do? What do they need to know to do what they need to do?
   - Choose content carefully.
     - Leave out any unnecessary information.
     - Limit to the who, what, when, where, and why.
   - Use effective links.
     - Links should describe the content they are linking to ("New Releases").
     - Don't use vague titles like "read more" or "click here" that don't provide the user with any information.
2. Organize your information: Put content in a logical order, from most important at the top to least important at the bottom, in an inverted pyramid.
   - Use headings to break up content.
     - Headings can be a question or statement.
     - Headings should be short.
     - Use keywords to highlight specific topics.
     - Use bold font and both upper- and lowercase letters, not all caps.
   - Use lists to highlight steps, requirements, or pieces of information.
     - Lists should be limited to three or fewer levels.
     - Lists should use parallel construction (like starting all bullet points with a verb or the same word tense).
     - Use standard bullets (and no more than two types of bullets per list).
   - Use tables to present complex material.
3. Make it easy to scan: Break content up so the user can scan through and find what they need.
   - Keep sentences and paragraphs short (no more than three to eight sentences per paragraph).
   - Keep sections short and chunk information into groups (no more than one topic per section).
   - Use plenty of white space between sections.
4. Write for, and to, your audience: Use language they understand to write content they feel personally connected to.
   - Don't use jargon or abbreviations (spell everything out).
   - Use the same terminology consistently throughout.

- Use positive language and the active voice.
- Write directly to the user ("you can check out new releases …") and use an informal, conversational tone.
- Use simple, plain language.

When the U.S. government made the use of plain language in federal documents into law, they also created a website with guidelines on how to write clearly, including the guideline to "pick the familiar or frequently used word over the unusual or obscure."[8] The plainlanguage.gov website includes a long list of complex words and their plain-language alternatives, including the "dirty dozen"—twelve words most likely to hinder your attempts at plain language found in table 1.2.

Typography

The typeface you decide to use on your website can have a big influence on the overall tone of your site. It is also a major factor in usability, as some fonts are considered more or less readable on some screens than others. General guidelines suggest that its best to stick to one or two typefaces; any more than that can make the site look inconsistent or unpolished. While it's generally best to stay away from overly fancy typefaces that often have poor readability, if you decide you want to use a decorative typeface, it should be limited to headings or illustrations, and not used for body text. A decorative typeface should also be paired with something more neutral and refined, like Helvetica or Arial, for the bulk of the text content.

There are several different classifications that are used to describe certain typefaces, or families, of fonts. Some common typeface classifications include:

- Serif: Uses serifs, or "feet," at the end of letter strokes and can have varying widths. Serif fonts have been used in printing for hundreds of years, and for many (though not all), they are thought to evoke traditional, warm, expensive, or old-fashioned connotations.
  Examples: Times New Roman, Garamond, Bodini
- Sans-serif: Typefaces without feet that have thinner strokes and a bigger height. Sans-serif fonts are known for being clear and legible, and they evoke more modern, hip, cold, and impersonal feelings.
  Examples: Helvetica, Proxima Nova, Futura, Open Sans
- Slab-serif: Typefaces that look sans-serif but have thick, block-like feet. Slab-serif fonts were once used in typewriters and are often used as display text.
  Examples: Courier, Clarendon, Archer, Memphis, Rockwell
- Script: Decorative typefaces that resemble handwriting and can look either very formal or very casual. Script fonts can be used to add flair or a sense of luxury to text, though they become less legible at smaller sizes.
  Examples: Pacifico, Parisienne, Allura, Lobster

Table 1.2 Examples of plain language alternatives.

Instead of	Write
Addressees	You
Assist, assistance	Aid, help
Commence	Begin, start
Implement	Carry out, start
In accordance with	By, following, per, under
In order that	For, so
In the amount of	For
In the event of	If
It is	(omit)
Promulgate	Issue, publish
This activity, command	Us, we
Utilize, utilization	Use

- Display: Somewhat decorative typefaces meant to be used in large sizes. Decorative and display fonts should be reserved for logos and headers, and never used for body text.
  Examples: Cooper Black, Bourton Font, Abril Fatface, Gilroy
- Monospace: Typefaces where all the letters take up the same amount of horizontal space. Monospace fonts resemble text from typewriters and early computer programming consoles.
  Examples: Courier, Roboto Mono, Inconsolata, Noto Mono

Many typefaces also have different weights available so that a single font can be used for different elements like headings and body text. Fonts usually come in weights including Light, Regular, Bold, Light Italic, Italic, and Bold Italic.

You may also want to consider whether or not the font you use is "web safe," meaning it's supported by the majority of web browsers and operating systems. Using a font that is not web safe can result in some users seeing something different from what you intended. One way to get around this is to host your own custom font; however, this can also slow down the speed of your website.

It would be much easier if there were one best font that should be used for all circumstances, but unfortunately, there is not one font that is best for all users. Studies have shown that some fonts that may be very readable for younger users might be less readable for older users whose eyesight is not as good. However, one study found that, on average, Garamond had the best readability, followed by Oswald.[9]

Some fonts you may want to consider are listed in table 1.3.

Color

Color is another area that can greatly impact the overall tone of your website. You may find that your color palette is already essentially chosen for you if your website needs to conform to the branding of a larger overall organization, such as a university. However, if you have the freedom to choose your own color palette, there are several considerations that may influence your choice.

For instance, color can impact a site's usability and accessibility. Ensure that the colors you choose, particularly the color of text against a background color, have enough contrast to meet accessibility guidelines. In addition, color should never be used to convey important information, unless it is in conjunction with text, since colorblind users may not be able to perceive the colors as you design them.

It is generally best to limit your color palette to three colors, as more can be distracting to users and disrupt the site's visual hierarchy. The rule to remember when using color is the 60-30-10 rule. The dominant color should be used for approximately 60 percent of the site. The secondary color should be used for around 30 percent. The final 10 percent should be an accent color.

When choosing a color palette, there are common color harmonies that are used to determine what colors go together. These color harmonies are determined by each color's location on the color wheel. The common color harmonies are:

- Analogous: Analogous colors are those that are next to each other on the color wheel, such as orange and red. An analogous color palette creates a low color contrast. Dunkin, Mastercard, and Instagram all use an analogous color palette.
- Complementary: Complementary colors are those that are directly opposite each other on the color wheel, such as orange and blue. Complementary color palettes create designs with high contrast. Brands that use a complementary color scheme include FedEx, SunBank, and Aviance.
- Split-complementary: A split-complementary color palette combines a color with colors next to its directly opposite color, such as purple, green, and orange. A split-complementary color palette softens the contrast that would be created by a complementary matchup. Trivago, Mozilla, and Fanta all use a split-complementary color scheme.
- Triadic: A triadic color palette uses three colors that are an equal distance from each other on the color wheel. An example of a triadic color palette would be the primary colors yellow, blue, and red. Triadic color schemes are vibrant and high contrast. One color should be dominant with the other two colors used as accents. Burger King and Tide both use a triadic color scheme.

Table 1.3 Types and examples of website fonts.

Typeface Description	Examples
Classic fonts	Avenir Clarendon Franklin Gothic Futura Garamond Gill Sans Gotham Helvetica Open Sans Times New Roman Verdana
Fonts designed for the web	Arial Calibri Corbel Libre Franklin Oswald Proxima Nova Roboto Source Sans Pro Ubuntu
Fonts designed for legibility	Frutiger Garamond Montserrat Morandi Noto Sans Optima Proxima Nova Roboto San Francisco Segoe UI
"Web safe" fonts	Arial Calibri Century Gothic Consolas Franklin Gothic Gill Sans Helvetica Lucida Sans Optima Tahoma Trebuchet MS Verdana

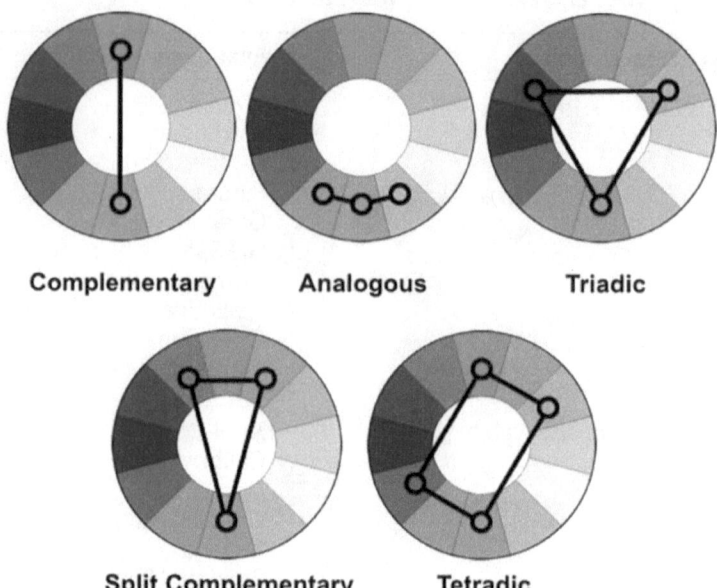

Figure 1.2 Examples of color harmonies. https://www.flickr.com/photos/80454089@N00/48458535436.

- Monochromatic: A monochromatic color palette uses just one color in a variety of different shades, such as using various shades of blue, or just black and white. A monochromatic color scheme can be very elegant and can be used to create a harmonious design. Monochromatic designs can have a different impact on the user depending on what color is used. Brands that use a monochromatic color scheme include Apple, Target, and Starbucks.

The main thing to remember is to use your chosen color palette consistently throughout the website, including maintaining the use of specific colors for certain types of elements. Color consistency will enhance the overall professionalism of the site and can help to create a memorable brand style.

Creating a Style Guide

When designing a website, it's important to also create a website style guide that will help any content creators adhere to the designated look and feel of the site. Without a thorough style guide, creators may make their own decisions about how to present content, which can quickly lead to inconsistencies in design and ultimately to a messy, disorganized website.

Ideally a style guide will include style direction on everything from buttons and icons to layout and spacing. A style guide should also cover colors, fonts, and overall tone or voice. Elements that should be detailed in the style guide include:

- Font style, size, color, and spacing for various types of text, including headings, subheadings, and body text.
- Color palette, including hex numbers, and what color should be used for what type of element (text, background, highlights, etc.).
- Language and terminology to use and to avoid; what tone to use.
- Rules around images, graphics, and audio/video content.
- Layout guidelines to follow.
- Navigation and menu type, look, labels, and placement.
- Buttons, including if they are part of the site's CSS framework, such as Bootstrap, and icons or if a specific icon set is being used, such as FontAwesome.
- How and when to use tables, captions, and data types (tabular versus used as a layout).
- Forms, input options, and labels.

CURRENT TRENDS IN WEBSITE DESIGN

While website conventions and best practices tend to stick around for a while, design trends are constantly evolving. Most trends are in practice for several years before they are replaced by new ideas. Not all design trends will be a good fit for your content or audience. Choose the ones that will enhance your website design and appeal to your users, and discard the rest.

The following list consists of fifteen website design trends that are current as of 2024.

1. Dynamic content and personalized interactions

    Personalized interactions use visitors' personal data to create a tailored experience. Users tend to spend more time on websites that feature interactivity, though this trend can be difficult to implement on some sites.
2. Storytelling

    The storytelling trend uses various methods to draw visitors into an interactive website experience through the use of branching narratives or interactive animation.
3. Textured/material design

    Textured or material design uses color and shadows to generate a textured effect. Material design can enhance user experience and the website's usability.
4. Retro design

Designs that evoke a sense of retro style through the use of nostalgic elements have become increasingly popular, including what is known as Y2K design (nineties retro) and Memphis design (eighties retro).

5. Glassmorphism

    Glassmorphism combines transparency, blur, and translucency to create a glassy effect. It can add depth to your site and is also a way to put focus on important content.

6. Dark mode

    Similar to Apple's dark mode, this trend features the use of low light or low contrast, drawing the user's eye directly to the main focus of the page. More sites are also using monochromatic black-and-white designs to make further use of this trend.

7. Full-page header/image header

    The full-page header is not a new concept but has become even more popular with the increased use of mobile devices. The full-page header, which can create brand consistency and draw a user's attention, and the image header, in which an image is incorporated into the header, provide visual appeal to users.

8. Custom illustrations

    The use of custom and hand-drawn illustrations to create unique imagery has become popular recently, including the use of animated design. Illustrations create a unique experience for users since the imagery is not seen elsewhere on the web, and illustrated images typically load faster than photographs, improving page load speed.

9. Parallax scrolling

    Parallax scrolling, an effect where the background moves at a different speed than the foreground image, was first popularized by Facebook and Twitter. It creates the impression of motion and depth and is visually engaging. Another similar trend is scroll-triggered animations, in which animations are activated as the user scrolls down the page.

10. Bold typography

    Kinetic, also called animated or interactive, typography has gained popularity, particularly to highlight important text or buttons on the page. Large or oversized text is also being used for its boldness and to make important text stand out.

11. Complex gradients

    Inspired by the rebranded Instagram logo, gradients are being used to create a sense of depth or dimension, and to add color to a website without being too distracting. Gradients can create an illusion of movement with minimal design. There are several online tools that can be used to generate gradients, such as Gradienta and CSS Gradient.

12. Bento box layouts

    A bento box design, named after the traditional Japanese lunchbox, uses compartmentalization and minimalism to divide content into distinct sections. It also tends to use elegant typography and plenty of white space. The layout is user-friendly and has more visual appeal than the typical grid layout.

13. Digital maximalism

    Digital maximalism is the trend of creating complex designs with multiple colors, textures, patterns, interactions, and fonts. Maximalism is in direct opposition to the usual best practice of simplicity in design. It is especially popular with websites targeted for younger audiences.

14. Use of Artificial Intelligence

    The use of AI has been a modern technology trend for a while, but it's now starting to become a popular way to automate design processes and create personalized user experiences. AI tools can be used to generate color palettes and optimize layout design. It can also be used to enhance accessibility and SEO. There are several online tools that use AI to create unique content, like Synesthesia, which lets you create custom AI avatars and voiceovers, as well as text-to-image generators like Midjourney.

15. Focus on UI/UX

    While all website design should be user-centered, there has been an increased focus recently on usability and user experience. This has led to more usability testing during the website design process and website elements that provide a unique but easy-to-use interface. While many of these recent trends are focused on visual engagement, a focus on usability ultimately leads to better website design and better overall user experience.

ADDITIONAL RESOURCES

- Blakiston, Rebecca. *Writing Effectively in Print and on the Web: A Practical Guide for Librarians. Practical Guides for Librarians, No. 30.* Lanham: Rowman & Littlefield, 2017.
- Krug, Steve. *Don't Make Me Think!: A Common Sense Approach to Web Usability.* 2nd ed. Berkeley, CA: New Riders Pub, 2006.
- Lynch, Patrick J. and Sarah Horton. *Web Style Guide, 4th Edition.* https://webstyleguide.com/.
- Nielsen Norman Group. https://www.nngroup.com/.
- Norman, Donald A. *The Design of Everyday Things.* New York: Basic Books, 2013.

NOTES

1. Stacy Ann Wittmann and Julianne Stam, *Redesign Your Library Website*, Santa Barbara, CA: Libraries Unlimited, 2016: 65.
2. Sarah Gibbons and Kelley Gordon, "Why Does a Design Look Good?" Nielsen Norman Group, March 7, 2021, https://www.nngroup.com/articles/why-does-design-look-good/.
3. Kelley Gordon, "The Golden Ratio and User-Interface Design," Nielsen Norman Group, October 31, 2021, https://www.nngroup.com/articles/golden-ratio-ui-design/.
4. Vitaly Friedman, "10 Principles of Good Web Design," *Smashing Magazine*, October 1, 2021, https://www.smashingmagazine.com/2008/01/10-principles-of-effective-web-design/.
5. Jakob Nielsen, "The Need for Web Design Standards," Nielsen Norman Group, September 12, 2004, https://www.nngroup.com/articles/the-need-for-web-design-standards/.
6. StatCounter, "Percentage of Mobile Devices Website Traffic Worldwide from 1st Quarter 2015 to 4th Quarter 2023," Statista, January 2024, https://www.statista.com/statistics/277125/share-of-website-traffic-coming-from-mobile-devices/.
7. U.S. General Services Administration, "Federal Plain Language Guidelines," Plainlanguage.gov, March 2011, https://www.plainlanguage.gov/guidelines/web/.
8. U.S. General Services Administration, https://www.plainlanguage.gov/guidelines/words/use-simple-words-phrases/.
9. Jakob Nielsen, "Best Font for Online Reading: No Single Answer," Nielson Norman Group, April 24, 2022, https://www.nngroup.com/articles/best-font-for-online-reading/?lm=pairing-typefaces&pt=article.

BIBLIOGRAPHY

Friedman, Vitaly. "10 Principles of Good Web Design." *Smashing Magazine*. October 1, 2021. https://www.smashingmagazine.com/2008/01/10-principles-of-effective-web-design/.

Gibbons, Sarah and Kelley Gordon. "Why Does a Design Look Good?" Nielsen Norman Group. March 7, 2021. https://www.nngroup.com/articles/why-does-design-look-good/.

Gordon, Kelley. "The Golden Ratio and User-Interface Design." Nielsen Norman Group. October 31, 2021. https://www.nngroup.com/articles/golden-ratio-ui-design/.

Nielsen, Jakob. "The Need for Web Design Standards." Nielsen Norman Group. September 12, 2004. https://www.nngroup.com/articles/the-need-for-web-design-standards/.

Nielsen, Jakob. "Best Font for Online Reading: No Single Answer." Nielson Norman Group. April 24, 2022. https://www.nngroup.com/articles/best-font-for-online-reading/?lm=pairing-typefaces&pt=article.

StatCounter. "Percentage of Mobile Devices Website Traffic Worldwide from 1st Quarter 2015 to 4th Quarter 2023." Statista. January 2024. https://

      www.statista.com/statistics/277125/share-of-website-traffic-coming-from-mobile-devices/.
U.S. General Services Administration. "Federal Plain Language Guidelines." Plainlanguage.gov. March 2011. https://www.plainlanguage.gov/guidelines/.
Wittmann, Stacy Ann, and Julianne Stam. *Redesign Your Library Website*. Santa Barbara, CA: Libraries Unlimited, an imprint of ABC-CLIO, LLC, 2016.

2

Trends in Library Website Design

What's popular to include on a library website or homepage changes over time, so before deciding on what content to feature on your homepage or what specific types of features to include, it's a good idea to take a look at a variety of other library websites and see what kind of content they feature on their homepage. Library websites can also vary depending on the library type as well. Looking across the websites of a wide variety of library types can give you more general ideas, but websites from those libraries within your industry may help to give you more specific ideas.

When deciding on what content to include on the homepage, library web developer Laura Solomon cautions against "kitchen sink syndrome," or the "unrealistic belief that everything libraries offer is equally important to visitors."[1] Solomon cites the top things that people generally come to the (public, in this case) library website for as to gain access to their account, to search the catalog, to find the library's phone number and address, and to search for program information.[2]

Other studies have named "address, telephone number, email address, contact forms, catalogue and database links, name of the director or library manager, and the last time the website was updated"[3] as the most essential homepage items to include. Some of the top needs for academic library website users include the library catalog, subject-specific resources, librarian and staff contact information, library hours, and interlibrary loan information.[4] However, the important thing to keep in mind during the design process is to "not overwhelm the user with an abundance of information," because like public library website users, "most students who visit the library are looking for something specific."[5]

So, what should be included on a library website, whether public, academic, or another library type? Some of the most common elements for library websites to include are:[6]

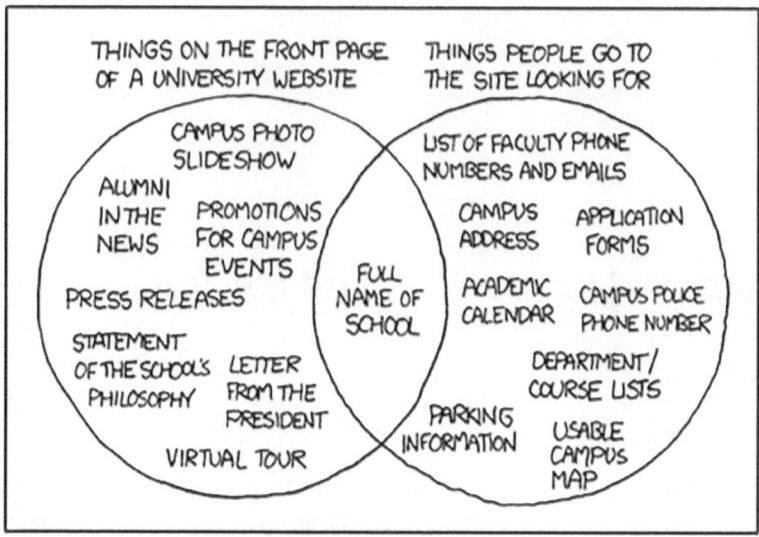

Figure 2.1 Comic from xkcd. https://xkcd.com/773/.

- Library hours
- Location information
- Contact information/staff directory
- News and upcoming events calendar
- Social media links**
- Circulation information
- Links to OPAC/digital/physical collections
- Ask a Librarian/help/feedback links
- Popular resources/quick links
- Chat/IM**
- Prominent search box/web-scale discovery access
- Account login/online renewal
- Personalization features

**While social media links are frequently found on library websites of all kinds, one study showed that only about 30 percent of academic library websites displayed links to social media accounts.[7] And while chat is overall a popular feature to include, especially for academic libraries, for public libraries in another study it was the least-common feature.[8]

Certain other elements are also frequently included, but only on websites of specific library types. Some of the frequently included elements on academic and public library websites specifically are:

Table 2.1   Common elements on academic and public library websites.

Academic Library Websites	Public Library Websites
Room reservations	New arrivals book feed
Links to subject guides	Staff picks
Virtual reference	Location finder
Instructional services	Names of board members
Interlibrary loan	Library mission statement

BEST PRACTICES

Just like the best practices commonly accepted for general website design, there are also best practices for library website design. As expected, there is some overlap in these best practices. Some of the best practices that are generally expected for modern library website design are:

- Responsive design: Just like for other modern websites, library websites should also use a responsive design. With so many people using mobile devices to access website content, not having a design that can be easily used on mobile will hinder your patrons' ability to engage with your site. While in the past it was common to create a specific mobile website separate from the desktop version, "current best practice is to build one web site that adapts to the viewing device."[9]
- Accessibility: Similar to responsive design, accessibility is a must for all websites, including library websites. Many library websites are considered government properties and are legally required to be accessible to all users. Even if it is not federally mandated, you can potentially discourage up to 25 percent of your patrons from using your website if it is not accessible.[10] See chapter 7 for more information on making your site accessible to all users.
- Security: All modern websites should also be secure against increasingly frequent cyberattacks as well as personal data breaches. Having a secure website instills trust in your patrons and is also important for maintaining control of the site. See chapter 8 on how to ensure your website is secure.
- Optimized images: Optimize images for size and compression to improve page load speeds. This is especially important as Google has discovered that more than half of all users will abandon a website if it takes more than three seconds to load.[11]
- Favicons: Using a favicon, the little icon that appears in the left corner of the browser tab next to the site's title, is optimal for many reasons, including that most professional websites use them and that not having one can make your website look unfinished or less professional. They are

also useful for users with multiple tabs open to easily find their way back to your site.
- Intuitive navigation: It almost goes without saying (but not really, see chapter 5) that having a simplified and intuitive navigation makes your site easier to use and easy for visitors to find what they need. When it comes to designing navigation, the best practice is to have no more than seven top-level menu items.[12]
- Prominent search box: A large number of users come to the library website to do research, so most library websites feature their search box prominently on the homepage. While some libraries choose to use a tabbed search box to offer search options for various separate resources (catalog, guides, discovery), libraries have increasingly "adopted a single search interface."[13] The library's main search box is generally placed front and center in the middle or near the top of the homepage.
- Library hours and contact information: This information is a must to include on the website's homepage, but generally libraries will include it somewhere in the header, footer, or another location that appears on every page of the site.
- Account login: Most patrons will appreciate easy access to their account and the ability to quickly find the link to log in. Many libraries include the account login link in the header of their website, where it is easily located.
- Quick links: While not an absolute must, most library patrons come to the website for a specific purpose, either to complete a task or to find information. Thorough user testing (see chapter 6 for information on user and usability testing) will give you solid information on what the most important tasks and information for your patrons are. Make it as easy as possible for patrons to find what they are looking for the most.
- Date of last update: Having the date of the website's last update somewhere on the homepage will go a long way toward instilling confidence about the accuracy and relevance of the information on your site. Users have more reason to trust the information on your website if they know it is updated with some regularity.
- Terminology and labels: Many studies have shown that library users don't understand common library terms and jargon that library staff often take for granted. Instead of library terminology, use clear, easy-to-understand terms to label your menu items and in other places throughout the site. It's also important to maintain consistency across the website and use the same terminology throughout, as frequently changing terms can be confusing to the user.

    Common terms used in navigation menus of academic library websites include:[14]
    - About
    - Services

- Collections
- Help
- Research
- Find
- Search

Common terms used in navigation menus of public library websites include:[15]

- Browse/borrow
- Events and programs
- Kids and teens
- Research
- Services
- About

What to Avoid

While knowing what features to include on the website is helpful, it is just as important to know what to avoid. Some of these should be avoided on any website, such as industry-specific jargon and acronyms; however, some of these things seem to be especially overused on library websites, where their inclusion can make it more difficult for your users to navigate and understand the site.

- Abbreviations and acronyms: You know what they mean because the library profession truly loves acronyms and you are used to seeing and using them, but library patrons generally have no idea. Spell these out at least the first time they are used on a page. Don't make your patrons turn to Google to find out what an ILL is and don't assume they will already know.
- Jargon: Similar to acronyms, library jargon is another problem that library websites tend to have. Terms like *database* and *circulation* are familiar to you, since you have been exposed to them from library school and likely use them frequently in your day-to-day work. But most library users are unfamiliar with these words, and clear, unambiguous language should be used instead.
- Contact forms: Sometimes websites will have a form that the user can submit instead of individual email addresses or other contact information, but "this approach is outdated and negatively impacts user experience and security."[16]
- Widgets: Widgets are a web 2.0 invention that conveniently allow you to dynamically pull information into your website from another domain. While they can be useful, consider carefully whether they will add enough to your website content to be worth the potential downsides, which

include slowing down your site and potentially not being accessible to users with disabilities.[17]
- Carousels: Like widgets, carousels can be useful for fitting more information into a smaller area of prime real estate on your homepage. However, carousels often look like advertisements to users and as such are frequently ignored. They can also slow down the site, create accessibility issues, and take control away from the user. The constant turnover of content can also be very frustrating to users.[18] If you find you must use a carousel, limit it to no more than four slides, and ensure the graphics look professional and the carousel works seamlessly on mobile devices.
- Taking control away from the user: It's never a good idea to take control away from the user. This can induce frustration and make users less likely to come to your site. Often this can also make your site less accessible, which is more reason to avoid it. Some of the ways a website can take control away from the user include:[19]
  - Auto-playing audio or video content
  - Opening links in new tabs or windows
  - Forcing users to provide more information than is necessary to perform an action
  - Autorotating carousel images
  - Disabling the browser's "Back" button

And What Not to Avoid

While you may have heard certain rules for things that you Definitely Should Not Do on a website, some of those rules persist from an earlier era and are no longer true for modern website design. For example:

- Scrolling is okay—While it may have been a best practice to avoid scrolling in the nineties and early 2000s, since the advent of smartphones, users have become very used to scrolling. They expect to scroll. You don't need to put everything "above the fold." It's still advisable to put the most important information at the top, and while "the fold" still exists, where it's located varies significantly based on the size of the user's device. Users will scroll down to see additional content if it's relevant to them; just be sure to avoid "false bottoms," or "false floors," that can make the user unaware there is more content below.[20]
- You don't need to follow the "three-click rule"—if it ever really existed. Users don't generally care how many clicks from the homepage something is. Additionally, due to Google search, many users will come into the site on a page that is not the homepage and may not require any additional clicks to get to the content they want. Arrange your site hierarchy in a way that makes the most sense and include bread-crumb navigation to let

users know where they are on the site, but don't limit the hierarchy to only three levels if more are needed.[21]

EXAMPLES OF GREAT DESIGN

When creating a new library website design, you may find inspiration by looking at what other libraries have done. There are many examples of great library website designs available to draw inspiration from. The following are some of the library websites that have recently been featured on "best of" library website lists.[22]

California State Library
https://www.library.ca.gov/
The California State Library website, shown in figure 2.2, is clean and modern with a simplified color palette and clearly labeled icons at the top that address common user needs. The search box is at the top center of the site above the hero image, and popular links are displayed as buttons below.

University of Pennsylvania
https://www.library.upenn.edu/
The University of Pennsylvania Library website, in figure 2.3, is simple with plenty of white space, making the site look clean and uncluttered. The main menu runs along the top using dropdowns with popular links found along the left side.

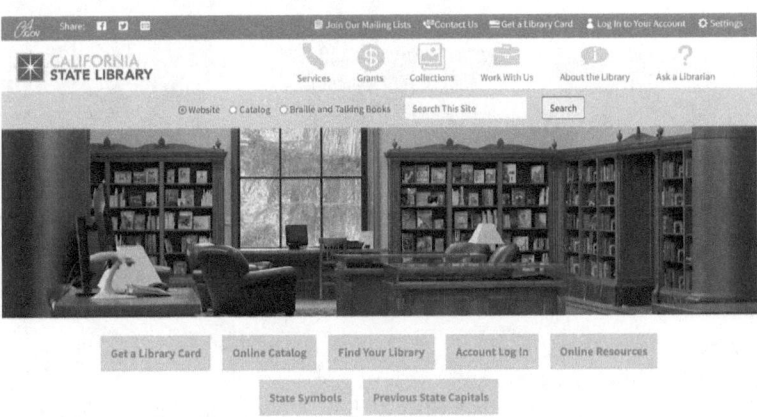

Figure 2.2   California State Library website. https://www.library.ca.gov/

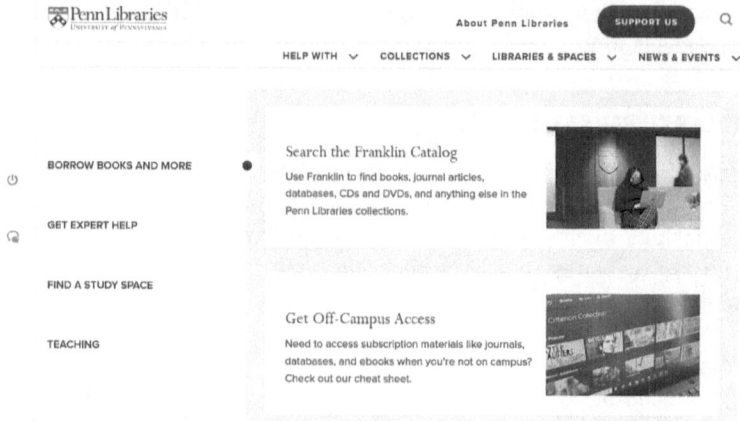

Figure 2.3   University of Pennsylvania website. https://www.library.upenn.edu/

Figure 2.4   Calgary Public Library website. https://calgarylibrary.ca/

Calgary Public Library
https://calgarylibrary.ca/
The Calgary Public Library website, in figure 2.4, features a simple monochrome header with the library's logo in the center and a more extensive menu hidden behind a hamburger menu icon in the upper left corner. The rest of the page uses simple, yet eye-catching icons and a coherent, attractive color palette. A pop-up custom chat feature aligns to the bottom left of the page.

Other Great Library Website Examples (2024)

Georgia State Library
https://library.gsu.edu/

Greenwich Library
https://www.greenwichlibrary.org/

Hinsdale Public Library
https://hinsdalelibrary.info/

Indiana State Library
https://www.in.gov/library/

New York Public Library
https://www.nypl.org/

Portland State University Library
https://library.pdx.edu/

University of Washington Libraries
https://www.lib.washington.edu/

Westerville Public Library
https://westervillelibrary.org/

ADDITIONAL RESOURCES

- Solomon, Laura. "Thinking Differently about Library Websites: Beyond Your Preconceptions." *Library Technology Reports 58*, no. 3 (2022). https://doi.org/10.5860/ltr.58n3.
- Unrein, Sabrina. "What Makes a Good Library Website?" Syracuse University School of Information Studies. May 20, 2019. https://ischool.syr.edu/what-makes-a-good-library-website/.
- Wittmann, Stacy Ann, and Julianne Stam. *Redesign Your Library Website*. Santa Barbara, CA: Libraries Unlimited, an imprint of ABC-CLIO, LLC, 2016.

NOTES

1. Laura Solomon, "Thinking Differently about Library Websites: Beyond Your Preconceptions," *Library Technology Reports 58*, no. 3 (2022): 9, https://doi.org/10.5860/ltr.58n3.
2. Solomon, 10.

3. Diane L. Velasquez and Jennifer Campbell-Meier, "Is Your Library Website Missing Essential Information?: A Comparison and Evaluation of Public Library Websites in Australia, Canada, and the United States," *Journal of Web Librarianship 16*, no. 3 (2022): 177, https://doi.org/10.1080/19322909.2022.2104777.
4. Brian Desmarais and Pamela Louderback, "Planning and Assessing Patron Experience and Needs for an Academic Library Website," *Journal of Library Administration 60*, no. 8 (2020): 966–77. https://doi.org/10.1080/01930826.2020.1820283; Scott L. Jones and Angie Thorpe, "Library Homepage Design at Medium-Sized Institutions," *Journal of Web Librarianship 8*, no. 1 (2014): 1–22, https://doi.org/10.1080/19322909.2014.850315.
5. Isabel Vargas Ochoa, "Navigation Design and Library Terminology," *Information Technology and Libraries 39*, no. 4 (2020): 3, https://doi.org/10.6017/ital.v39i4.12123.
6. See appendix A for a complete list of sources used to determine both popular features and best practices for modern library websites.
7. Daniel Moody, "Patterns of Two-Year College Library Websites," *Journal of Web Librarianship 16*, no. 3 (2022): 157, https://doi.org/10.1080/19322909.2022.2100556.
8. Amy VanGoethem, "Public Library Websites in the Reaching Across Illinois Library System: A Webometric Examination," *SLIS Connecting 12*, no. 1 (2023): 9, https://doi.org/10.18785/slis.1201.05.
9. David Comeaux, "Web Design Trends in Academic Libraries—A Longitudinal Study," *Journal of Web Librarianship 11*, no. 1 (2017): 12, http://dx.doi.org/10.1080/19322909.2016.1230031.
10. Solomon, 25.
11. Solomon, 21.
12. "8 Tips to Improve Your Library's Website Design," Piola, March 27, 2018, https://meetpiola.com/8-tips-to-improve-your-librarys-website-design/.
13. Comeaux, 2.
14. "8 Tips."
15. Terry W. Brandsma and David Comeaux, "Behind the Scenes of Academic Library Website Design: Patterns and Trends from 2012 to the Present," NCLA Biennial Conference (2019), https://libres.uncg.edu/ir/uncg/f/T_Brandsma_Behind_2019.pdf; Comeaux.
16. Sabrina Unrein, "What Makes a Good Library Website?," Syracuse University School of Information Studies, (2019): 15, https://ischool.syr.edu/what-makes-a-good-library-website/.
17. Solomon, 18.
18. https://shouldiuseacarousel.com/.
19. Solomon, 26.
20. Amy Schade, "The Fold Manifesto: Why the Page Fold Still Matters," Nielsen Norman Group, February 1, 2015, https://www.nngroup.com/articles/page-fold-manifesto/.
21. Solomon, 18–19.
22. Ron Johnson, "25 Best Library Websites." CyberOptik, accessed March 6, 2024, https://www.cyberoptik.net/blog/25-best-library-websites/; Aigars Silkalns, "19 Best Library Website Design Inspiration 2024," Colorlib, January 3, 2024, https://

colorlib.com/wp/library-website-design/; "The 25 Best Library Websites for 2019," Piola, May 2, 2019, https://meetpiola.com/the-25-best-library-websites-for-2019/.

BIBLIOGRAPHY

"8 Tips to Improve Your Library's Website Design." Piola. March 27, 2018. https://meetpiola.com/8-tips-to-improve-your-librarys-website-design/.

Brandsma, Terry W., and David Comeaux. "Behind the Scenes of Academic Library Website Design: Patterns and Trends from 2012 to the Present." NCLA Biennial Conference (2019). https://libres.uncg.edu/ir/uncg/f/T_Brandsma_Behind_2019.pdf.

Comeaux, David. "Web Design Trends in Academic Libraries—A Longitudinal Study." *Journal of Web Librarianship 11*, no. 1 (2017): 1-5. http://dx.doi.org/10.1080/19322909.2016.1230031.

Desmarais, Brian, and Pamela Louderback. "Planning and Assessing Patron Experience and Needs for an Academic Library Website." *Journal of Library Administration 60*, no. 8 (2020): 966-77. https://doi.org/10.1080/01930826.2020.1820283.

Moody, Daniel. "Patterns of Two-Year College Library Websites." *Journal of Web Librarianship 16*, no. 3 (2022): 147-64. https://doi.org/10.1080/19322909.2022.2100556.

Ochoa, Isabel Vargas. "Navigation Design and Library Terminology." *Information Technology and Libraries 39*, no. 4 (2020): 1-15. https://doi.org/10.6017/ital.v39i4.12123.

Schade, Amy. "The Fold Manifesto: Why the Page Fold Still Matters." Nielsen Norman Group. February 1, 2015. https://www.nngroup.com/articles/page-fold-manifesto/.

Solomon, Laura. "Thinking Differently about Library Websites: Beyond Your Preconceptions." *Library Technology Reports 58*, no. 3 (2022). https://doi.org/10.5860/ltr.58n3.

Unrein, Sabrina. "What Makes a Good Library Website?" Syracuse University School of Information Studies. May 20, 2019. https://ischool.syr.edu/what-makes-a-good-library-website/.

VanGoethem, Amy. "Public Library Websites in the Reaching Across Illinois Library System: A Webometric Examination." *SLIS Connecting 12*, no. 1 (2023). https://doi.org/10.18785/slis.1201.05.

Velasquez, Diane L., and Jennifer Campbell-Meier. "Is Your Library Website Missing Essential Information?: A Comparison and Evaluation of Public Library Websites in Australia, Canada, and the United States." *Journal of Web Librarianship 16*, no. 3 (2022): 165-83, https://doi.org/10.1080/19322909.2022.2104777.

APPENDIX A

Sources Used to Determine "Popular Features" and "Best Practices" for library websites

"8 Tips to Improve Your Library's Website Design." Piola. March 27, 2018. https://meetpiola.com/8-tips-to-improve-your-librarys-website-design/.

Abifarin, Fasola P., and Shaka A. Imavah. "Design Evaluation of Academic Library Websites in Nigeria." *African Journal of Computing and ICT 11*, no. 3 (2018): 12–32. https://afrjcict.net/wp-content/uploads/2017/08/vol11no3sept18pap2journformnumbered.pdf.

Bartlett, Harry. "Recent Trends in Library Website Design." BI. October 5, 2020. https://bi.studio/blog/library-website-design-trends.

Becker, Danielle A. "Best Practices of Library Mobile Website Design: A Literature Review." *College & Undergraduate Libraries 21* (2014): 167–87. https://doi.org/10.1080/10691316.2014.877736.

Boateng, Frank, and Yan Quan Liu. "Web 2.0 Application's Usage and Trends in Top US Academic Libraries." *Library Hi Tech 32*, no. 1 (2014): 120–38. https://doi.org/10.1108/LHT-07-2013-0093.

Brandsma, Terry W., and David Comeaux. "Behind the Scenes of Academic Library Website Design: Patterns and Trends from 2012 to the Present." NCLA Biennial Conference (2019). https://libres.uncg.edu/ir/uncg/f/T_Brandsma_Behind_2019.pdf.

Chow, Anthony, Michelle Bridges, and Patricia Commander. "The Website Design and Usability of US Academic and Public Libraries." *Reference & User Services Quarterly 53*, no. 3 (2014): 253–65. https://www.jstor.org/stable/pdf/refuseserq.53.3.253.pdf.

Comeaux, David. "Web Design Trends in Academic Libraries—A Longitudinal Study." *Journal of Web Librarianship 11*, no. 1 (2017): 1–15. http://dx.doi.org/10.1080/19322909.2016.1230031.

"Creating a Simple Library Website." Alaska State Libraries, Archives & Museums. July 14, 2021. https://lam.alaska.gov/webcreate/design.

Desmarais, Brian, and Pamela Louderback. "Planning and Assessing Patron Experience and Needs for an Academic Library Website." *Journal of Library Administration 60*, no. 8 (2020): 966–77. https://doi.org/10.1080/01930826.2020.1820283.

Florio, Nancy. "Five Steps to a User-Friendly Library Website." AISL News. May 21, 2019. https://aislnews.org/tag/library-website/.

Johnson, Ron. "25 Best Library Websites." CyberOptik. Accessed March 6, 2024. https://www.cyberoptik.net/blog/25-best-library-websites/.

Jones, Scott L., and Angie Thorpe. "Library Homepage Design at Medium-Sized Institutions." *Journal of Web Librarianship 8*, no. 1 (2014): 1–22. https://doi.org/10.1080/19322909.2014.850315.

Kumar, Vinod, and Jivesh Bansal. "Qualities of a Library Website: Evaluating Library Websites of New IITs." *International Journal of Information*

Dissemination and Technology 4, no. 3 (2014): 283–88. https://www.researchgate.net/profile/Jivesh-Bansal/publication/281578900_Qualities_of_a_Library_Website_Evaluating_Library_Websites_of_New_IITs/links/55ee77c808ae0af8ee1a1152/Qualities-of-a-Library-Website-Evaluating-Library-Websites-of-New-IITs.pdf.

Liao, Kai, and Feng Li. "Construction of Modern University Library Website (CMULW) Based on User Needs." *IOP Conf. Series: Materials Science and Engineering 630* (2019): 1–5. https://doi.org/10.1088/1757-899X/630/1/012028.

"Library Website Design Tips." Compete Now. September 26, 2022. https://startcompeting.com/blog/library-website-design-tips/.

Moody, Daniel. "Patterns of Two-Year College Library Websites." *Journal of Web Librarianship 16*, no. 3 (2022): 147–64. https://doi.org/10.1080/19322909.2022.2100556.

Ochoa, Isabel Vargas. "Navigation Design and Library Terminology." *Information Technology and Libraries 39*, no. 4 (2020): 1–15. https://doi.org/10.6017/ital.v39i4.12123.

Shah, Abdul Hakim, and Sharif Hossain. "Public University Library Websites in Bangladesh: Features, Contents and Maintenance Issues." *Library Philosophy and Practice* (2022): 1–19. https://digitalcommons.unl.edu/libphilprac/7233/.

Silkalns, Aigars. "19 Best Library Website Design Inspiration 2024." Colorlib. January 3, 2024. https://colorlib.com/wp/library-website-design/.

"The 25 Best Library Websites for 2019." Piola. May 2, 2019. https://meetpiola.com/the-25-best-library-websites-for-2019/.

Unrein, Sabrina. "What Makes a Good Library Website?" Syracuse University School of Information Studies. May 20, 2019. https://ischool.syr.edu/what-makes-a-good-library-website/.

Vacek, Rachel. "Library Websites of the Future." SLA Texas Chapter Fall Meeting (2014). http://hdl.handle.net/10657/1315.

Vacek, Rachel. "The Changing Nature of Web Design and User Expectations, and How Libraries Can Respond." Houston Area Law Librarians Meeting (2015). http://hdl.handle.net/10657/1306.

VanGoethem, Amy. "Public Library Websites in the Reaching Across Illinois Library System: A Webometric Examination." *SLIS Connecting 12*, no. 1 (2023). https://doi.org/10.18785/slis.1201.05.

Velasquez, Diane L., and Jennifer Campbell-Meier. "Is Your Library Website Missing Essential Information?: A Comparison and Evaluation of Public Library Websites in Australia, Canada, and United States." *Journal of Web Librarianship 16*, no. 3 (2022): 165–83, https://doi.org/10.1080/19322909.2022.2104777.

3

Content Management Systems

A content management system (CMS) is software that manages content for display on a website. Content management systems separate the content from the layout and design of the website, allowing for the easy reuse of both content and design elements. This enforces a "consistency of design across all pages while at the same time increasing efficiency by making the maintenance of the content itself less technically challenging."[1] Due to this separation, multiple users can create and edit content on the website collaboratively, even if they don't have any technical or coding skills. About two-thirds of websites on the internet rely on a content management system, with over 40 percent currently using WordPress.[2]

A content management system will usually have reusable elements, such as the website header, footer, and navigation menu, which can be applied across multiple pages on the website. This eases maintenance by providing a central location to edit code or content, reflecting those changes across the entire site rather than having to edit each page individually. This is especially helpful for large sites that may have several hundred pages of content. The site's CSS code, which dictates the look and feel of the entire website, is also centrally managed, so any changes can be applied to the entire site at one time. Many content management systems also include additional features, such as search engine optimization (SEO), a responsive design, and accessibility features.

Content management systems will often have a WYSIWYG (What You See Is What You Get) editor, where users can drag and drop items and edit content directly on the page rather than having to work with any HTML code. A WYSIWYG editor allows anyone to create, update, and publish content without the need to do any coding. Most WYSIWYG editors also have the option to view the page's source code, which can be edited directly if desired.

Content management systems offer multiple benefits for organizations and are currently the most common way to manage website content. Some of the benefits of using a CMS rather than maintaining a hand-coded site include:

- Simplicity: Using a CMS allows even tech novices to be able to add content and update design elements on a website, so a library doesn't necessarily need to have skilled developers on staff to use one. A CMS also manages all of a website's written content, digital assets, layout, and design within a single web-based platform.
- Workflow management: Most CMS platforms allow you to appoint different roles to multiple users, such as admin, author, or editor, each with their own level and type of permissions. Many content management systems can also be used to implement workflows for the publication of new content, such as an approval process, to maintain the integrity of the site. This is especially useful if there will be multiple content creators.
- Ease of customization: Many content management systems are highly customizable, and this can be done without significant coding knowledge through the use of plugins, templates, and extensions. These features let you quickly and easily update the look and feel of your website.
- Easy updates: Since content is separated from the architecture of the site, it is easy to make changes or updates to content without affecting anything else on the website. Multiple people can also be permitted to make content changes, potentially streamlining the website update process.
- SEO: Many content management systems have SEO features integrated into the platform, or available through a plugin or other tools. SEO tools help get your site noticed and ranked on popular search engines, making your content easier for users to find.
- Consistency: With layout and design elements centrally managed, it is easier to maintain consistency of color, font, and layout throughout the website. Certain content elements can also be used repeatedly across the site, such as in the site's header, footer, and navigation menu, meaning these elements only need to be updated in a single location to reflect changes across the entire site.
- Cost: There are many open-source content management systems that are free to download and use, which can be a huge cost savings if you have skilled staff with the knowledge to set up and customize the platform. Without the requisite in-house skills, however, you may need to consider the cost of hiring additional personnel, or a technical consultant, along with the cost of web hosting.
- Security: Many content management systems provide various security features, such as firewalls, SSL certificates, authentication, or expert security review, to make it easier to keep your website secure from hackers or malware.

- Integrations: Content management systems can often be integrated with third-party software, such as SSO authentication. Some systems, like LibGuides, include full integration with other compatible modules like a ticketing system, calendar, and booking system with the website.
- Digital asset management: Content management systems offer a centralized location to store and organize digital assets, often in cloud-based storage, making them easily accessible to staff.

Many modern content management systems run on a LAMP stack, which stands for:

- **L**inux (operating system)
- **A**pache (web server)
- **M**ySQL (database)
- **P**HP (coding language)

However, some may use a WAMP (Windows) or MAMP (Mac) stack or a different web server, such as Nginx. There are also alternative database systems that can be used instead of MySQL, such as MariaDB or MongoDB, and alternative coding languages, like Perl and Python, can be used instead of PHP. When choosing a CMS, it is important to ensure that the platform is compatible with whichever tech stack you'll be using.

CMS ARCHITECTURE

Content management systems are generally made up of a front end and a back end. The front end is the client-side, which consists of everything a website visitor sees on the site. The back end, or the server-side, consists of the server, the database, and the application itself. The back end is where website content is stored, updated, and structured.

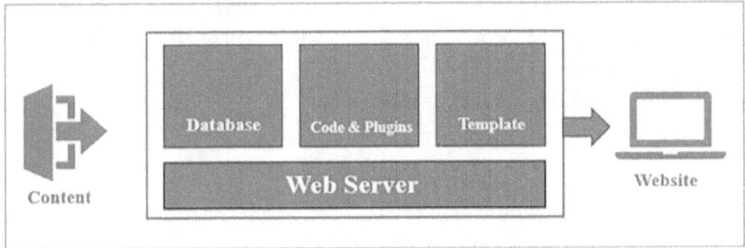

Figure 3.1 Diagram of a traditional content management system. Brighid M. Gonzales.

There are different types of CMS architectures based on how the front-end and back-end components are arranged, each with different benefits and use cases. The main types of CMS architectures include:

Coupled

A coupled (also known as a conventional or traditional) content management system is one in which the front and back ends are joined. In a coupled CMS, creating a webpage, hosting it, and publishing it all happen from the application's dashboard. Coupled content management systems are easy to manage, and content can be designed and published quickly with pre-built templates. However, they can sometimes be restrictive if you are limited to just the templates and features provided by the CMS. Having the front and back ends combined can also leave the site more vulnerable to security issues.

Coupled CMSs: Drupal, WordPress.org, Joomla!

Decoupled

In a decoupled content management system, the front and back ends are separated and operate independently of one another. A decoupled CMS uses an API (application programming interface) to facilitate communication between each component. By using a decoupled CMS, the work of the website developers and that of the content creators are kept separate, making the system less vulnerable to security issues. However, this architecture is more complex and is sometimes more costly to manage than a coupled CMS.

Decoupled CMSs: Parse, Ponzu, Contentstack

Headless

A headless CMS is similar to a decoupled CMS, with the front and back ends managed separately. However, in a headless CMS, there is not a defined front end, and content can be published to multiple other channels in addition to the website. These other channels could include a web app, or an iOS or Android native app. As with a decoupled CMS, content from a headless CMS is delivered through the use of an API. Headless content management systems allow for a great deal of flexibility with site design; however, each front end must be built individually from scratch. This adds to the complexity, and ultimately the cost, of the platform.

Headless CMSs: Strapi, Contentful, Sanity

Hybrid

Hybrid content management systems are some combination of coupled, decoupled, and headless architectures. In a hybrid CMS, the front and back ends are separate, but the front end is managed through a specific presentation layer, delivered through an API. By using a hybrid CMS, content can be delivered to multiple channels, but through a single front-end framework. Hybrid content management systems can make developing and sharing content easier; however, managing that content across different platforms can also make it more complicated.

Hybrid CMSs: Sitecore, Zesty, Kontent

SaaS

SaaS stands for software-as-a-service and is a service model in which a vendor provides access to a hosted content management system as a licensed service. SaaS makes things extremely easy since both the platform itself and the hosting service are provided for you. You only need to go in and customize and add content. SaaS content management systems often offer limited customization options since the back-end processes are all managed by the hosting provider; however, using them can greatly simplify the entire process.

SaaS CMSs: LibGuides, BiblioWeb, WordPress.com

Table 3.1 Types of CMS architectures.

Architecture	Structure	Best For	Examples
Coupled	Joined front and back ends	Blogs Personal websites Small businesses	Drupal WordPress Joomla!
Decoupled	Separate front and back ends	Large sites with high traffic	Parse Ponzu Contentstack
Headless	No single front end	Enterprise businesses	Strapi Contentful Sanity
Hybrid	Separate front and back end with single front end presentation	Organizations wanting unlimited flexibility in content delivery	Sitecore Zesty Kontent
SaaS	Managed by the service provider	Organizations wanting web hosting and CMS management provided by the vendor	LibGuides BiblioWeb WordPress.com

CHOOSING A CMS

When deciding on a content management system, the first step is to define your library's requirements for the new system. These requirements will be specific to your organization's use case, but there are several features you will need to consider in your decision, including the system's architecture, cost, and ease of use.

In an article on the process of selecting a CMS for an academic library, Elizabeth Black included the following list of requirements the author's library gathered to make their selection.[3] While your organization's requirements may differ in some places, this list may be a useful place to begin thinking about your needs. Although this list was created for an academic library, most of the requirements will also apply to public and other library types.

Content Creation and Ownership Requirements

- Separation of content and presentation
- Web-based GUI content editing environment (intuitive, easy to learn)
- Metadata for each webpage
- Multi-user authoring
- Integration of RSS feeds
- Accommodation of multiple content providers
- Accommodation of multiple content types (text, images, videos, etc.)
- Ability to display tabular data/tables
- Ability to host forms

Content Management Requirements

- Link maintenance
- Repurposing elements
- Access controls
- Robust reporting features

Publishing Requirements

- Content preview
- Production of RSS feed
- Centrally controlled templates and style sheets
- Use of Unicode to display non-Roman characters
- Extensibility
- Personalization options

Presentation Requirements

- ADA and W3C accessibility compliance
- HTML validation

- Usability
- Dynamic navigation
- Search capability
- Mobile friendliness
- Multi-browser compatibility
- Fast page load times
- SEO optimization

Administration Requirements

- LAMP stack
- Robust documentation
- Scalability
- Necessary tech skills available in-house

DECISION FACTORS

In the process of defining your requirements and researching CMS options, there are a variety of factors that need to be considered. While multiple factors will influence your decision, the most important ones for libraries tend to be ease of use, flexibility, and cost.[4] When comparing cost, it is important to consider the total cost of ownership. While open-source software may be "free," you will also need to consider the cost of web hosting, as well as potential development costs if in-house staff are not already familiar with the software or the coding language in which the software is written. At times, the total costs for open-source and licensed software platforms may be roughly equivalent due to the additional costs that free open-source software can require.[5]

The following factors should be taken into consideration when deciding on a new CMS:

- Ease of use: Is the system easy to set up and use, even without extensive technical knowledge? Will you need to hire a consultant, or someone experienced with the software, or will you be able to do the work in-house? Once set up, is the software intuitive and user-friendly for potential users?
- Flexibility: How customizable is the system? Are you limited in layout and design choices? Are there enough plugins or extensions to provide the customizations you need?
- Cost: Is the system open-source and free to use, or is it only available through a subscription? Will you need to pay separately for hosting, or is that included in the cost? Are the templates, plugins, and extensions you need available for free, or do they have an additional cost? Consider total cost of ownership even after the system is in place.

- Templates: How many and what kind of pre-designed templates are available to use? Are there library-specific templates available? Can you easily create your own custom templates if needed?
- SEO features: What SEO features are built in or available through plugins or extensions? Are you able to create customized page titles and metadata? Are SEO features kept up-to-date along with changes in search engine algorithms?
- Security features: Is security managed by the system/vendor, or will you be fully responsible for securing the site? Does the vendor provide regular security patches and updates? If the CMS is open-source, is the code still being developed and kept up-to-date with patches for new and ongoing security concerns? Does the vendor have a dedicated security team in place to review code and manage issues? Are firewalls, SSL certificates, and multi-factor authentication options included?
- Content editing: Does the system offer a live preview through a WYSIWYG editor, and can users add and update content without needing to use HTML? If the interface is drag-and-drop, do users also have access to directly edit the source code if needed?
- Customer/Community support: What kind of support is available? Does the vendor offer live support, or will you be dependent on community support only? How large and active is the user community? How robust is the available documentation?
- Scalability: Will the system allow you to scale your website as it grows and accumulates more content? Will it be able to handle an increase in user traffic if needed? What kind of server hardware is used or required? Can server resources be easily increased or decreased according to changing needs?
- Mobile responsiveness: Does the system have mobile responsive design built in? What type of framework is being used, if any (i.e., Bootstrap)? Will content display the way you intend it to, no matter what size the user's browser is? Will users on a tablet or cell phone be able to easily use all the features on your site?
- Accessibility: Does the system manage accessibility and adherence to ADA guidelines and requirements? Do drag-and-drop or WYSIWYG interfaces validate HTML to current standards? Can alt-text, text alternatives, or transcripts be stored with images, audio, or video content? Are available themes and templates created with accessibility in mind?
- Integration: Can the system integrate with other tools as needed, such as email marketing, customer relationship management software, analytics, or authentication systems? Is the integration seamless and supported by the vendor?
- Analytics: Are analytics collected by the software, or can you easily add tracking to gather analytics for the site? Can the analytics data available

give you the information needed for assessment, such as number of page views, unique visitors, and referring URLs?
- User administration: Can users be given various permissions and roles based on what work they need to do within the system? Can user groups be established for permission-based access?

SYSTEM COMPARISONS

There are currently over eighty different content management systems on the market, though the top ten platforms account for over 85 percent of the market share. Some of the top platforms, like Shopify and Squarespace, however, are geared toward e-commerce sites and may be less appropriate for managing a library website than other options.

Among the top ten platforms are popular open-source options, including Drupal, Joomla!, and WordPress (wordpress.org), which are also frequently used by libraries. Popular licensed options include Wix, TYPO3, and hosted WordPress (wordpress.com). While you may want to consider additional options outside of this short list, table 3.2 compares these popular content management systems on important factors such as price, security, ease of use, flexibility, and customer support.

CONTENT MANAGEMENT SYSTEMS FOR LIBRARIES

While Drupal, Joomla!, and WordPress are some of the most popular content management systems overall, in libraries, Drupal, WordPress, and LibGuides are the most frequently used.[6] However, many libraries are required to use the same CMS as their parent institution and may not be able to pursue other options. Other libraries, particularly those at larger institutions, may be able to implement their own content management system separate from the institution.

During the search for a content management system, some libraries have found that no existing systems meet all their requirements, and instead they opt to build their own custom application.[7] While this option necessitates having expert developers on staff and may not be practical for all, or even most, libraries, it does result in a system that will meet every one of your needs.

Open-Source CMS Options

For libraries that don't have the resources to create their own original content management system, but do have technically inclined employees on staff, open-source systems can be a good option. Drupal, Joomla!, and WordPress are all robust options that allow for varying degrees of customization, while

Table 3.2 Comparison of popular content management systems.

CMS	Pricing	Security	Ease of Use	Flexibility	Customer Support
Drupal	$0/month	Security team regularly reviews and fixes issues	Requires some coding skills	Highly customizable	Strong community support
Joomla	$0/month	User manages website security	Requires some coding skills	Customizable	Strong community support
TYPO3	$0/month	User can customize security options	Requires some coding skills	Customizable	Some vendor support
Wix	$16/month	Managed by vendor	No coding knowledge required	Limited customization	Live vendor support
Wordpress.com	$4/month	Managed by vendor	No coding knowledge required	Limited customization	Live vendor support
Wordpress.org	$0/month	User manages website security	Requires some coding skills	Highly customizable	Strong community support

also requiring varying degrees of technical expertise to use to their fullest potential.

Drupal

Drupal has long been a popular open-source option for content management, has a large and active user community, and continues to be developed and regularly updated. While it can be difficult to install and set up for someone without either extensive development experience or previous Drupal experience, it is extremely flexible and customizable. Drupal uses themes to determine the layout and design of the site and offers extended features and functions through the addition of modules. "Drupal's flexibility, robust architecture, modularity, and open-source license allow libraries to extend and customize it to meet their individual needs,"[8] making it particularly appealing to larger libraries that require maximum flexibility. Drupal's user community has been called its greatest asset[9] and there are library-specific user groups as well. Over two hundred public libraries and over one hundred academic libraries, as well as several special libraries, school libraries, and consortia, are listed as Drupal users on the Drupal Groups—Libraries page.[10]

Joomla!

Joomla! provides less flexibility than Drupal, but it is also considerably easier to configure, with a simple, user-friendly interface. However, some coding knowledge is also required to fully customize a Joomla! website. Instead of themes, Joomla! uses templates to control a site's look and feel, and while it offers good functionality out of the box, it can also be extended with the addition of plugins. Despite its overall popularity, Joomla! is less frequently used as a content management system for libraries than either Drupal or WordPress, perhaps due to the lack of library-specific templates available. However, its ease of use may make it a viable option for small- or medium-sized libraries.[11]

WordPress

WordPress requires the least technical knowledge of these popular open-source systems and is considered fairly intuitive to use. Like Drupal, WordPress uses themes to determine a site's layout, look, and feel. There are thousands of WordPress themes available for free or for purchase, or someone with knowledge of PHP could easily create their own custom theme. WordPress also uses plugins to extend functionality, and technical users can create their own custom plugins as well. WordPress has a strong presence in libraries and has been called "a perfect fit" for "many types of libraries and educational organizations—large and small."[12]

Library-Specific CMS Options

In the past decade or more, several library-specific content management systems have been created to cater to the unique needs of library websites. Many of these grew out of other library-specific software, such as LibGuides, which was initially built to host library-created research guides, and BiblioWeb, created by the same company that makes the BiblioCore OPAC. LibGuides is arguably the best-known library CMS with 7,500 institutional customers.[13] LibGuides and BiblioWeb are both licensed options, but there is also Omeka, which provides a library-centric open-source option. These options are described below.

LibGuides

While LibGuides was initially created by Springshare as a SaaS product to support the online publication of library research guides, it can also be used as a content management system for hosting a library's website. This has been shown to be a viable option for smaller libraries, though few large libraries use it for that purpose,[14] preferring something more robust. Because it is a SaaS platform, you have less control over the customization of the back end, but it also makes website integration with other Springshare products, such as LibAnswers, LibCal, and LibWizard, especially easy. Springshare also offers a great deal of customer support. While LibGuides customers are traditionally academic libraries, they also serve public libraries, special libraries, school libraries, medical and law libraries, and consortia.

BiblioWeb

BiblioWeb is a library SaaS platform developed by BiblioCommons that includes a drag-and-drop interface and easy integration with other Biblio-Commons products, such as BiblioCore (OPAC) and BiblioEvents. BiblioWeb comes with customizable templates, or users can create their own designs. BiblioWeb is popular among public libraries, particularly those that already subscribe to other BiblioCommons products.

Omeka

Omeka is an open-source platform that can serve as a content management system, a digital asset management system, and a collections management and exhibition software package. Many libraries use the free Omeka software to host digital collections or online exhibits, though it may not scale well for an entire website. Omeka uses the Dublin Core metadata standard, and it can use linked open data to connect digital objects to the semantic web. It also includes templates to describe items for directly sharing with the Digital Public Library of America. In addition to the freely downloadable Omeka S software, there is also a paid hosted version called Omeka.net.

ADDITIONAL RESOURCES

- Austin, Andy, and Christopher Harris. "Drupal in Libraries." *Library Technology Reports 44*, no. 4 (May/June 2008).
- Dobbs, Aaron W., and Ryan L. Sittler, eds. *Integrating LibGuides into Library Websites*. Lanham: Rowman & Littlefield, 2016.
- Goodman, Amanda L. *The Comparative Guide to WordPress in Libraries: A LITA Guide*. Chicago: ALA TechSource, 2014.
- Jones, Kyle M.L., and Polly-Alida Farrington. *Learning from Libraries That Use WordPress: Content-Management System Best Practices and Case Studies*. Chicago: American Library Association, 2013.
- Librarian's Toolbox. "Content Management Systems (CMS)." https://librarytoolbox.wordpress.com/behind-the-scene-solutions/cms/.
- Pope, Elizabeth. "Content Management Systems for Library Websites." TechSoup. April 6, 2015. https://blog.techsoup.org/posts/content-management-systems-for-library-websites.
- Varnum, Kenneth J. *Drupal in Libraries (The Tech Set #14)*. Edited by Ellyssa Kroski. Chicago: ALA TechSource, 2012.

NOTES

1. Elizabeth L. Black, "Selecting a Web Content Management System for an Academic Library Website," *Information Technology and Libraries 30*, no. 4 (2011): 185. https://doi.org/10.6017/ital.v30i4.1869.
2. Munider Adavelli, "Exploring the Latest CMS Statistics and Its Impact on Content Management," January 2, 2024. https://techjury.net/blog/cms-statistics/.
3. Black, 186–87.
4. Ruth Sara Connell, "Content Management Systems: Trends in Academic Libraries," *Information Technology and Libraries 32*, no. 2 (2013): 51. https://doi.org/10.6017/ital.v32i2.4632.
5. Connell, 53.
6. Connell, 48.
7. Black, 186.
8. Karen Coombs, "Drupal Done Right," *Library Journal 134*, no. 19 (2009): 32. https://www.libraryjournal.com/.
9. Andy Austin and Christopher Harris, "Drupal in Libraries," *Library Technology Reports* 44, no. 4 (2008): 7. https://journals.ala.org/index.php/ltr/issue/view/117.
10. Drupal Groups, "Libraries Using Drupal," updated November 10, 2023, https://groups.drupal.org/libraries/libraries.
11. Ellen Bahr and Matt Speed, "Creating Library Websites with Joomla: Not Too Big, Not Too Small, Just Right," *Code4Lib Journal 12* (2010). https://journal.code4lib.org/articles/4226.
12. Kyle M. Jones and Polly-Alida Farrington, "Using WordPress as a Library Content Management System," *Library Technology Reports 47*, no. 3 (2011): 12. https://journals.ala.org/index.php/ltr/article/view/4277.

13. Springshare, accessed February 14, 2024, https://www.springshare.com/.
14. Connell, 53.

BIBLIOGRAPHY

Adavelli, Munider. "Exploring the Latest CMS Statistics and Its Impact on Content Management." January 2, 2024. https://techjury.net/blog/cms-statistics/.

Austin, Andy, and Christopher Harris. "Getting started with Drupal." *Library Technology Reports 44*, no. 4 (2008). https://journals.ala.org/index.php/ltr/issue/view/117.

Bahr, Ellen, and Matt Speed. "Creating Library Websites with Joomla: Not Too Big, Not Too Small, Just Right." *Code4Lib Journal 12* (2010). https://journal.code4lib.org/articles/4226.

Black, Elizabeth L. "Selecting a Web Content Management System for an Academic Library Website." *Information Technology and Libraries 30*, no. 4 (2011): 185–89. https://doi.org/10.6017/ital.v30i4.1869.

Connell, Ruth Sara. "Content Management Systems: Trends in Academic Libraries." *Information Technology and Libraries 32*, no. 2 (2013): 42–55. https://doi.org/10.6017/ital.v32i2.4632.

Coombs, Karen. "Drupal Done Right." *Library Journal 134*, no. 19 (2009): 32. https://www.libraryjournal.com/.

Drupal Groups. "Libraries Using Drupal." Updated November 10, 2023. https://groups.drupal.org/libraries/libraries.

Jones, Kyle M., and Polly-Alida Farrington. "Using WordPress as a Library Content Management System." *Library Technology Reports 47*, no. 3 (2011). https://journals.ala.org/index.php/ltr/article/view/4277.

Springshare. Accessed February 14, 2024. https://www.springshare.com/.

W3Techs. "Usage of Content Management Systems." Accessed February 13, 2024. https://w3techs.com/technologies/overview/content_management/all.

4

Content Strategy

INVENTORIES, AUDITS, AND NEEDS ASSESSMENT

Before you can begin designing a new website, you need to know what content you plan to have, or in the more likely event of a website redesign, what content you already have. Having a full accounting of all the content on your website is an important step in the design planning process. The design itself should be driven by the content, as that is ultimately what your website visitors come to find.

Content strategy is often associated with the business world, but all organizations with web content can benefit from doing at least some content strategy during a design or redesign process. Libraries especially tend to have a great deal of content, and with sometimes small staffs, library websites may not be given the ongoing attention they deserve, which can quickly result in outdated or irrelevant content proliferating the site. Content strategy can make the difference between having a well-organized, frequently used website, and a website full of outdated, unplanned content that patrons find difficult to navigate.

Terms like *content inventory*, *content auditing*, and *needs assessment* are all parts of the content strategy process. *Content strategy* is "the ongoing practice of planning for the creation, delivery, and governance of useful, usable, and effective content about a particular topic or set of topics."[1] Part of the process of content strategy involves identifying content you have (content inventory), evaluating content you have (content auditing), and identifying content you need (needs assessment).

Information architect Chris Detzi suggests there are four reasons to perform a content audit:

1. To reveal the true scale of the website's content
2. To clarify and refine the project scope

3. To facilitate strategic discussions about design objectives and direction
4. To establish a common language for the team to use throughout the project[2]

The terms *content inventory* and *content audit* are sometimes used interchangeably, but they are each distinct parts of the process, although they are often done in tandem. A content inventory, sometimes referred to as a quantitative audit, is a process in which you collect a list of every piece of content on your website, including pages, links, images, videos, audio content and documents. A content inventory can be done for the entire website, or it can be scoped to a specific part of the website. For a full website redesign project, inventorying the entire website is a good idea. However, partial content inventories can be helpful as part of an ongoing maintenance process.

Content auditing, sometimes referred to as a qualitative audit, is the evaluative part of the process. Using the content inventory as a starting point, an audit is conducted to evaluate the content for things like relevance, accuracy, and accessibility, as well as general web-based standards and the library's overall goals. While a content inventory will identify the content you currently have, a content audit can help you determine which content is already in good shape, which content needs to be remediated, and which content is no longer necessary.

While quantitative and qualitative audits are the most frequently used, there are other types of audits that can also be performed. Content strategy expert Ahava Leibtag identifies three additional audit types: mapping audits, rolling audits, and thin slice audits.[3] A mapping audit presents the content in the form of a site tree, which allows you to see the relationships between content and the level of depth and breadth contained in the overall site content. A rolling audit is essentially a never-ending audit process, wherein you audit one section of the site at a time until all the content has been audited, then return to the beginning and start auditing again. A thin-slice audit is similar to a rolling audit in that you limit the audit to a small section of the site, giving you a "thin slice" view of the content. Thin-slice audits can be useful when auditing very large websites or redesigning only a small section of the site. Leibtag recommends combining audit types when possible, to get a true sense of the content on the site.

PHASES OF CONTENT STRATEGY

There are four phases of content strategy identified by the expert UX consulting group Nielsen Norman.[4] The four phases of content strategy include:

1. Planning
    The planning phase will help determine the organization's content strategy by identifying things like the website's audience and goals, what

topics will be covered, who will be responsible for the content on the website, and what CMS will be used to manage the website. The planning phase encompasses the content inventory, the content audit, user research, and needs assessment.

2. Creation

The creation phase involves creating the content, as well as determining guidelines for the ongoing creation and addition of new content. The creation phase includes determining the editorial and legal standards the website will use, style guides, best practices, tone and voice, and content formats.

3. Maintenance

The maintenance phase involves content governance and establishing a timeline for performing ongoing content inventory and audits, deciding how changes and additions will be initiated and who will be responsible for implementing them, and evaluating and adjusting the content and overall content strategy as needed.

4. Unpublishing

The unpublishing phase involves removing outdated or irrelevant content to ensure that the website only contains the most recent and most useful information. Some things that will need to be determined include who decides why and when to remove content, whether unpublished content should be archived and for how long, and if there are outside links to the content that will need to be updated or redirected.

In addition to the four phases of content strategy, content strategists also make use of the "content lifecycle,"[5] a five-stage framework that provides an iterative process for designing and creating content. The five stages of the content lifecycle include:

1. Audit and Analysis: User research, competitive analysis, performance analysis, and content inventory and evaluation.
2. Strategy: Defining ownership, developing taxonomy, defining voice and tone, and determining workflows for the production of new content.
3. Plan: Planning the site migration project, assigning tasks, customizing the CMS, and planning metadata.
4. Create: Writing content, producing assets, formulating governance model, and search engine optimization (SEO).
5. Maintain: Plan for ongoing evaluation of the site, including regular audits and determining what metrics will be used to measure performance.

BEST PRACTICES FOR CONTENT CREATION

When creating website content, there are several generally recommended best practices that can help you to create relevant, effective content that patrons will find informative and easy to understand. Some of the best practices for content creation on the web are listed below.

Writing

- Use simple and plain language that your users will find easy to understand.
- Keep sentences and paragraphs short (no more than twenty words per sentence and five sentences per paragraph is a good guideline).
- Use style guidelines to establish vocabulary terms, tone, and voice, so that writing throughout the site remains consistent, even if written by different employees.
- Use personal and friendly language, such as referring to the reader as "you" rather than "the student" or "the patron," and keeping the tone informal.
- Use the active voice.
- Get to the point. Don't include unnecessary or irrelevant information that may take users' focus away from what they are trying to find.

Formatting

- Use content "chunking" to break large amounts of text into more easily digested sections.
- Use bullet points and numbered lists to make information easier to scan.
- Include white space to help reduce information overload and a cluttered appearance.
- Avoid using underlines, bold, italics, and all caps as much as possible.

Organizing

- Put the most important information first (at the top) in an inverted-pyramid structure.
- Use headings and subheadings to organize information on the page.
- Don't duplicate content on multiple pages.

CONDUCTING A NEEDS ASSESSMENT

Before you can start designing a new website, you'll first need to determine your goals for the site. Usually this will involve determining what your users' goals are when they visit your site. While a needs assessment might seem like an unnecessary step, "twenty hours spent on a needs assessment can easily save forty hours of development time during the building of the site."[6] Oftentimes librarians think they know what their users want and need, but the only way to know for sure is to ask them. User research regularly provides surprises and contradicts assumptions made by the researchers. Using objective user research data to determine user needs can also prevent or end arguments between stakeholders about what is really needed on the site. Performing user research allows for data-driven decision-making when it comes to designing the new website.

Content strategist and user experience expert Kristina Halvorson[7] identifies the need for both internal and external analysis when conducting a needs assessment. Internal analysis involves gathering feedback and requirements from people internal to the organization, such as librarians, directors, and other stakeholders. Internal analysis can be gathered through interviews, group discussions, questionnaires, or surveys.

External analysis involves examining external impact factors that can influence decisions about the website. There are various methods for gathering external analysis depending on the factor involved. External impact factors can include:

Trends and Best Practices

You likely spend some time on the internet and regularly visit a variety of websites. As you browse the internet, pay attention to some of the elements being used by current, popular websites. You may recognize current trends in website design when you start to see them regularly. You may also get new ideas about different ways to use certain elements, such as new navigation techniques or interactive elements.

Advances in Technology

Advances in technology can also change the way your website may be designed or built. For example, the advent of smartphones and tablets created the need for responsive design, accessibility standards for websites have evolved over time, and new website frameworks change the underlying technology being used in web design.

Trade Journals and Industry Associations

Trade journals and associations may not directly influence library website design, but you may find articles or stories about current library website practices published in the professional literature, and various library associations may have guidelines on their websites, such as ALA's "Library Privacy Guidelines for Library Websites, OPACs, and Discovery Services."

Competitors

While you might consider other libraries more as peers than as competitors, looking at the websites of other libraries, particularly those of a similar type, size, or community, can provide you with ideas for how other libraries are organizing and presenting their content. Not everything that another library does with their website is likely to be considered a best practice or good website design; however, they can provide a glimpse of current trends in library websites or ideas for how other libraries generally present things like their online catalog or discovery interface.

Users

Your users are likely to, and should, have the greatest impact on your external analysis of what your library website needs to have. After all, the website was created for them, to allow them to find the resources and information they need from your library. Your users will have specific goals and needs when they visit your site, and it is important that you know what they are so that the website you design is as relevant and easy to use as possible.

Getting to know your users' needs can be an involved process. However, there are many methods that can be used to gather data about your users and their needs. Some commonly used methods for gathering user research and other user-focused data include:

- User interviews: Usually conducted one-on-one, user interviews can be done in person, over the phone, or online, and they allow for in-depth, structured conversation as well as follow-up questions.
- Focus groups: Focus groups allow you to conduct an in-depth discussion with multiple patrons at one time and can be an efficient way to gather information from multiple users at once.
- Surveys: Surveys are an easy way to collect a large amount of data quickly from many different users, including those who may not visit the library in person.
- Website analytics: Website metrics, such as those provided by Google Analytics, can provide information on which pages are most and least visited, how much time visitors spend on certain pages, and their trajectory through the website.
- Search and keyword analytics: Analyzing the keywords that people search for on your website can tell you what information is difficult for them to find, if your patrons use different terminology than what is used on your site, or if users are looking for information that is not included on the site.
- User interaction analytics: Many libraries collect information from user interactions, such as questions asked at the reference desk or through chat, that may provide information about some user needs.

It may be helpful in some cases to create personas and user journeys to guide your assessment of user needs. Personas are fictional users that represent a major user group of your website, such as students, teens, or users with disabilities. The data used for creating your personas should come from the information you gathered doing user research. A persona clearly defines the person and their basic demographics, as well as what they need and expect from the website. A user persona should answer experience and content questions about your user, as well as about their needs, motivations, and behaviors. Personas can be as detailed as you want; however, even a brief sketch can be useful for developing their user journeys.

A user journey (or customer journey) is a series of steps a user takes to complete a goal or task. User journeys should describe major tasks that a persona wants to complete. For example, the persona of a teen patron may have a user journey that describes how that person would use the website to find upcoming events for teens. A student persona might have a user journey that maps out how the person would find and download an article for a research project.

Sometimes a journey map is also created to visualize the user's journey. "Mapping out a current journey versus an optimized journey can help show gaps in current content and point to areas for improvement."[8]

CONDUCTING A CONTENT INVENTORY

Before you can decide what to do with your content, you will need to know exactly what content you have. This is where the content inventory comes in. "A content inventory is a quantitative assessment of all the content on a website—a list of all the pages, images, and other files that make up the content set as well as data associated with those files, such as content type and metadata."[9] A complete content inventory can provide you with information such as the exact number of pages on the site, what topics are covered, what formats are included, and the content's place in the site hierarchy. The content inventory must be performed before the content audit can take place. It provides the foundation for the website's content strategy, governance, and improvement of the overall user experience, including how the content is structured and labeled, whether it is accessible and findable, and how it is navigated.

A content inventory is generally created by using a spreadsheet of some kind and can include almost any kind of information about the content on the site. You will want to inventory and record information about each:

- Page
- Link
- Image
- Audio/Video file
- Document/PDF
- Downloadable file
- Form
- Widget

To scope the inventory to a reasonable size, it will help to begin by deciding what information to collect and how it will help you when you move forward to the audit process. It is not always possible or necessary to collect every possible piece of information, but some of the types of information that can be collected are listed below. Including some basic information is important, but you will need to determine what data to include.

- Name/Title of page
- Location/URL
- Brief description
- Keywords
- Author/Owner
- Subject matter/Topic
- File format
- File size
- Creation date
- Last updated date
- Audience

This information should be collected and documented in a spreadsheet such as Excel. For smaller sites, it should be possible to complete the inventory manually; however, there are also a number of tools that can be used to help start or automate a content inventory.

CONTENT INVENTORY TOOLS

Content inventories do not need to be done in Excel; however, it is usually easiest to keep track of the information in some kind of spreadsheet software. Some options for creating a content inventory spreadsheet include:

Name/Title	URL	Author/Owner	Subject/Topic	Format	Creation Date

Figure 4.1 An example of a content inventory spreadsheet. Brighid M. Gonzales.

- Microsoft Excel
    https://www.microsoft.com/en-us/microsoft-365/excel
    Microsoft Excel is the industry leader for spreadsheet software, and it's very likely that you already have access to it through your organization. Excel can be used as either a desktop application or online. The Office 365 version allows for sharing and collaboration.
- Google Sheets
    https://www.google.com/sheets/about/
    Google Sheets is another widely used spreadsheet software that is available freely online through your Google account. Sheets is an online software that allows for sharing and collaboration in real time.
- LibreOffice Calc
    https://www.libreoffice.org/discover/calc/
    Calc is a free, open-source software spreadsheet program that is part of the LibreOffice suite, a free office suite based on OpenOffice. LibreOffice can be used on Windows, Mac, and Linux.
- Notion
    https://www.notion.so/help/tables
    Notion is a productivity app that can be used to create spreadsheets but is also integrated with other tools, such as task management, project tracking, and notetaking. There is a free version as well as several subscription tiers.

For very large websites, it may be necessary or helpful to perform a content inventory using some kind of automated tool. Some tools that can be used to automate the content inventory process include:

- Smartocto (formerly Content Insight)
    https://smartocto.com/
    Created as a "smart content analytics system" for editorial newsrooms, Smartocto can provide detailed content inventory reports, site mapping, and quality analysis. Smartocto is proprietary software and requires a subscription, though they do offer a free demo.
- Content Mapping by Siteimprove
    https://www.siteimprove.com/
    Siteimprove is a web-monitoring tool that can be used to provide content inventory reports, site mapping, and quality analysis and requires a subscription to use.
- DYNO Mapper
    https://dynomapper.com/
    DYNO Mapper is a content-strategy tool that can be used to create sitemaps, conduct content audits, and visualize relationships between

content. They offer a free trial period followed by three tiers of subscription plans.
- Screaming Frog
    https://www.screamingfrog.co.uk/seo-spider/
    Screaming Frog is an SEO agency based in the UK. Its SEO Spider web crawling software can be used to generate a comprehensive URL list with metadata like page title, description, headings, and alt text, as well as to identify duplicate content and broken links. SEO Spider is free; however, they offer a paid version if you need to crawl more than 500 URLs or have access to advanced features.
- Your own CMS
    If your website is on a content-management system, it should be able to provide you with a list of all of the pages on your site, which can help you get started in the inventory process.

CONDUCTING A CONTENT AUDIT

Once you've completed a content inventory and know exactly what content your website contains, you can perform a content audit to evaluate that content. This information can be used to determine necessary actions and revisions, content that is no longer needed, or content that should be improved or added. A thorough content audit can help you determine which content performs best, along with multiple other metrics.

Before you begin, it may be useful to develop a rubric to evaluate the content in your audit. This will ensure consistency in your evaluation across content. A very simple evaluation rubric that can be used is ROT, where content is evaluated for **R**edundancy, **O**utdatedness, and **T**riviality. ROT can be especially useful for websites that have been around for a long time and may have accumulated a great deal of content that has not been recently evaluated.

A more thorough content audit rubric that can be used is Rahel Bailie's RAITES rubric,[10] which evaluates content based on whether it is:

- **R**elevant
- **A**ccurate
- **I**nformative
- **T**imely
- **E**ngaging
- **S**tandards-Based

Content strategy expert Paula Land also recommends evaluating content on quality, effectiveness, and legal issues.[11] These factors cover most of the criteria that can help you determine the state of your current content and how you need to move forward. Some of the criteria you may want to consider during your audit is listed in table 4.1.

To evaluate these criteria, you will need to gather data from several key sources. For example, to know if a certain page is frequently visited by users, you'll need to have statistics for how many times the page was visited within a specific time period, as well as similar statistics about other pages on the site to compare. In order to know whether content is easy to find, you may need to perform usability testing on the site. Some sources of data that your content can be evaluated against during an audit include:

- Performance analytics: Number of page views, referral links, visitor pathways, frequency and duration of visits.
- Accessibility guidelines: Formal guidelines for meeting accessibility requirements, such as WCAG and ADA guidelines.
- Style and editorial guidelines: Organizational guidelines for writing and styling written content, general web best practices guidelines.
- Link checking: Automated link checking software can be used to find broken links on the site.
- Search logs: Logged data on the number of searches performed in a given time frame and keywords used.
- Direct feedback: Emails or submissions from a feedback or "contact us" form on the website.
- User feedback: Feedback from users regarding the site gathered through surveys, interviews, or focus groups.
- Usability testing: Data gathered about the usability and user-friendliness of the website through user testing.

Once content has been thoroughly evaluated, the next step is to create an action plan for what to do with it. A new column can be added to the spreadsheet to track what action will be taken for each piece of content, including:

- Keep: Content is in good shape and should be kept as is.
- Remove: Content is unnecessary or irrelevant and should be removed.
- Improve: Content is relevant but needs to be edited for currency, accuracy, readability, consistency, usability, accessibility, or other issues (be specific).
- Consolidate: Content is duplicated or can be combined with other content.

You can also use the content audit along with the user-needs assessment to perform gap analysis to identify necessary but missing content. Then develop an action plan for creating it, including who will be responsible for creating the content, in what formats the content will be created, and where it belongs

Table 4.1 Criteria for auditing website content.

Criteria	Assessment
Relevance	• Content is on topic. • Content communicates the organization's key messaging. • Content provides information users are looking for. • Page is frequently visited by users.
Currency	• Content is up-to-date. • Content covers topics of current interest to users.
Accuracy	• Content provides correct information to users. • Links are functional and go to the correct location.
Engagement	• Tone is friendly and personal. • Language is user-centric. • Messaging is audience-appropriate.
Readability	• Content uses headings, bullet points, and lists. • Content is divided into easily digestible chunks. • Language is simple, clear, and concise.
Consistency	• Tone and voice are consistent throughout site. • Terminology is used consistently. • Files use regular naming conventions. • Content is not duplicated. • Formatting is consistent.
User-Friendliness	• Content is easy to find; navigation is intuitive. • Site is mobile-friendly. • Page hierarchy is logical.
Accessibility	• Content uses unbiased language. • Content meets ADA recommended guidelines, such as WCAG.

on the site. Missing content should be tied directly to user and organizational goals and needs.

Content Auditing Tools

While content auditing is a process that generally requires human involvement to make decisions regarding the content, there are several tools you can use to help you gather information that will aid in making those decisions. Some online tools that you can use during a content audit include:

- Google Analytics
  https://analytics.google.com/
  Google Analytics is a popular platform for gathering analytical data on a website. Google Analytics can track web activity, such as the number of views for each page, bounce rate, and how traffic gets to the page. Google Analytics can be used for free, with optional paid features also available.

- Google Search Console
    https://search.google.com/search-console/about
    Google Search Console is another of Google's web-analytics tools that provides information about search queries and web crawls, as well as site speed reports and page experience reports. It can also be used to gather a list of internal and external pages linking to the site. Like Analytics, Search Console is free to use.
- Hotjar
    https://www.hotjar.com/
    Hotjar is an online analytics tool that offers heatmaps, visitor recordings, and form analysis. Hotjar offers qualitative metrics in comparison to Google Analytics' quantitative metrics. Hotjar can be used for free, with optional paid features also available.
- SEMrush
    https://www.semrush.com/
    SEMrush is a suite of tools created for marketing and SEO purposes. It offers keyword research, competitor analysis, site audits, and online visibility insights. SEMrush can be used for free, but it also offers paid plans with additional features.
- WAVE
    https://wave.webaim.org/
    WAVE is a free online tool that can audit your site against accessibility standards, such as WCAG (Web Content Accessibility Guidelines); however, you will also need to manually check for accessibility errors since automated tools are not able to catch them all.

ADDITIONAL RESOURCES

- Blakiston, Rebecca. "Developing a Content Strategy for an Academic Library Website." *Journal of Electronic Resources Librarianship 25*, no. 3 (2013): 175–91.
- Halvorson, Kristina. *Content Strategy for the Web*. Berkeley, CA: New Riders, 2012.
- Kissane, Erin. *The Elements of Content Strategy*. New York, NY: A Book Apart, 2010.
- Land, Paula Ladenburg. *Content Audits and Inventories: A Handbook for Content Analysis*. Laguna Hills, CA: XML Press, 2014.

NOTES

1. Anna Kaley, "Content Strategy 101," NN/g Nielsen Norman Group, November 13, 2022. https://www.nngroup.com/articles/content-strategy/.

2. Ahava Leibtag, *The Digital Crown: Winning at Content on the Web*. Amsterdam: Morgan Kaufmann, 2013, 201.
3. Leibtag, 201–02.
4. Kaley.
5. "Content Strategy Basics," Usability.gov, accessed January 4, 2024, https://www.usability.gov/what-and-why/content-strategy.html.
6. Ben Seigel, "A Comprehensive Website Planning Guide (Part 1)," *Smashing Magazine*, February 20, 2018. https://www.smashingmagazine.com/2018/02/comprehensive-website-planning-guide-part1/.
7. Kristina Halvorson, *Content Strategy for the Web, Second Edition*. Berkeley, CA: New Riders, 2012.
8. Paula Ladenburg Land, *Content Audits and Inventories: A Handbook for Content Analysis*. Laguna Hills, CA: XML Press, 2014, 53.
9. Land, xi.
10. Land, 31.
11. Land, section II.

BIBLIOGRAPHY

"Content Strategy Basics." Usability.gov. Accessed January 4, 2024. https://www.usability.gov/what-and-why/content-strategy.html.

Halvorson, Kristina. *Content Strategy for the Web*. Berkeley, CA: New Riders, 2012.

Kaley, Anna. "Content Strategy 101." NN/g Nielsen Norman Group. November 13, 2022. https://www.nngroup.com/articles/content-strategy/.

Land, Paula Ladenburg. *Content Audits and Inventories: A Handbook for Content Analysis*. Laguna Hills, CA: XML Press, 2014.

Leibtag, Ahava. *The Digital Crown: Winning at Content on the Web*. Amsterdam: Morgan Kaufmann, 2013.

Seigel, Ben. "A Comprehensive Website Planning Guide (Part 1)." *Smashing Magazine*. February 20, 2018. https://www.smashingmagazine.com/2018/02/comprehensive-website-planning-guide-part1/.

5

Information Architecture and Navigation Design

When it comes to designing a website, one of the most important aspects is how the content of the site is organized, and the ways in which users are able to access that content. "Websites have as little as 25–35 seconds to convince users that the information they are looking for is available,"[1] and how easy the website is to navigate has a direct correlation on how user-friendly the site is overall.

The way content is structured and labeled on the website refers to the website's information architecture (IA). It is the structural backbone of the website and helps inform other design decisions going forward. While information architecture and navigation design are sometimes thought of as interchangeable, they are different, but related, concepts. Navigation design is one aspect of information architecture and makes up one of the core components of information architecture, along with the website's organization, labeling, and search systems. Navigation is what leads the user through the website to the content they need and is essential to a good website design. But navigation design cannot begin until the website's information architecture has been created.

User experience and information architecture experts Louis Rosenfeld, Peter Morville, and Jorge Arango, authors of one of the classic texts of the field, *Information Architecture for the World Wide Web*, defined three interrelated concepts they called the "information ecology" that inform a website's information architecture.[2] These concepts include:

Users: The people who are seeking out the information on your website, including their behavior, experiences, and information needs;

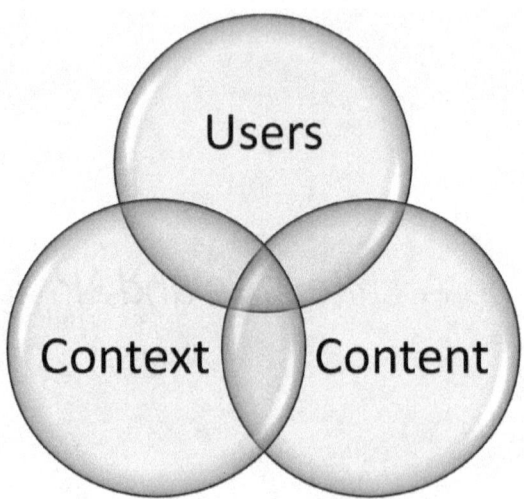

Figure 5.1 Venn diagram of the three interrelated parts of information architecture. Brighid M. Gonzales.

Context: The environment in which the user engages with the content, including when, why, and how; and
Content: The information available on the website with which a user interacts.

Because library science involves categorizing, labeling, and locating resources, the field easily lends itself to the processes of user experience, including information architecture. However, IA is also influenced by cognitive psychology, including the concepts of cognitive load, mental models, and decision-making.[3]

Cognitive load refers to the amount of information a person can process at one time. When designing navigation and website content, it's important to factor in the average person's cognitive load to avoid overloading them with too much information. Keeping designs simple and organizing content into logical hierarchies can help balance the cognitive load a website places on the user.

Mental models are a person's individual version of something they hold in their mind and use to make sense of the world. Mental models can help people to understand and interact with different aspects of the world around them, but when a product doesn't match up to a user's mental model, it can cause confusion and difficulty. Website designs that adhere to common web conventions and standards are a better match with most users' mental models and make finding information on the website much easier and more intuitive for the user.

Decision-making is a cognitive process that factors into how users make decisions as they navigate a website. Providing additional information at key decision points and creating a logical framework for information can ease the decision-making process for users. This can help you to build trust with your users, leading to a better overall user experience.

THE EIGHT PRINCIPLES OF INFORMATION ARCHITECTURE

There are eight principles of information architecture devised by information architect and UX designer Dan Brown in 2010. These principles act as a set of "guidelines based in universal truths that provide a sketch of what makes any information architecture good."[4] The eight principles of information architecture are:

1. Objects
    The object principle considers content as a dynamic and changing thing with its own lifecycle, behaviors, and attributes. Consider the content needed for your site and how each section relates to the others.
2. Choices
    The choices principle asserts that each website page should offer a number of meaningful choices to the user but keep the range of choices focused on a particular task so that users are not overwhelmed.
3. Disclosure
    The disclosure principle is also focused on not overwhelming the user by showing them only enough information to give them context about any further information available. The most important information should be disclosed first, as in Google's use of "featured snippets" that highlight a relevant piece of information about the user's search along with a link to find more information.
4. Exemplars
    The exemplar principle suggests describing content categories by providing examples of the content, such as images and diagrams that go along with a written tutorial.
5. Front Doors
    The front door principle asserts that there are multiple entry points to any website and at least half of your users may arrive to your website through a page other than the homepage. With this assumption, any navigation should be accessible through every page on the website.
6. Multiple Classifications
    The multiple classifications principle suggests that a website should offer users multiple ways to navigate the website, such as having a menu bar at the top of the page as well as including bread-crumb navigation on individual pages.
7. Focused Navigation
    The focused navigation principle states that the navigation scheme should be consistent throughout the website. Navigation schemes that

change from one page of the website to another are confusing for users and make finding information more difficult.
8. Growth
    The growth principle asserts that you will likely have more content in the future than you have now, and therefore the structure of the website should be able to accommodate this potential growth.

THE MAIN COMPONENTS OF INFORMATION ARCHITECTURE

Along with the concept of an information ecology, created by Rosenfeld, Morville, and Arango, the authors also defined four main components of information architecture: organizational systems, labeling systems, search systems, and navigation systems.[5] The combination of these four components make up a website's information architecture.

- Organizational systems
    Organizational systems are the way that you categorize or classify information. Some examples of common organizational systems include:
    - Hierarchical: Information is organized by importance.
    - Sequential: Information is organized in a logical path or in steps.
    - Alphabetical: Information is organized in alphabetical order.
    - Chronological: Information is organized by time.
    - Topical: Information is organized by subtopics within a larger topic.
    - User segmented: Information is organized by specific groups of users, such as students, faculty, or staff.
- Labeling systems
    Labeling systems are the way that you title sections of content, including headings and subheadings. Labels should be easy for users to understand and use common terminology they are familiar with. Labels give users context for where they can find the information they need.
- Search systems
    Search systems allow users to search by keywords and can include a search engine as well as filters. Search systems give users more control and can gather data from multiple areas of the website into one place. Users are familiar with search options and will likely expect to see one if the website is very large.
- Navigation systems
    Navigation systems give users a way to browse through the website to access the information they need. There are various types of navigation systems, including navigation bars (menu bars), bread crumbs, pagination, primary navigation, and sub-navigation.

DESIGNING INFORMATION ARCHITECTURE

There are many different methods that can be used to create an information architecture, and these methods can be used in combination or as a series of steps. The basic steps for designing an information architecture include:

1. Conduct a content inventory: Review all of the content on your existing website and consider any additional information that needs to be included on the site. This is also a good time to analyze your website content to identify duplicate information, outdated information, or information that is no longer relevant or useful.
2. Perform user research: User research should be conducted early in the design process to gather information about how your users experience and navigate the website. User research can include things like surveys and focus groups, as well as creating user personas to identify the different types of users of your website, what they need, and how they use information. Card sorting tests can also be used at this stage to determine how different types of content on the site are related to each other for users, how they categorize information, and even the type of terminology, or labels, they expect for different types of content.
3. Group the information: Using the information gathered in the user research stage, along with the content inventory you conducted, you can now group the various content on your website into chunks to create categories that will be used to house the different types of content.
4. Develop the labels: User research should also be used to develop the labels for your website, or the titles of each category of content. Labels should be short, easy to read, familiar to users, and unique enough to separate the various types of content clearly. In your user research, you will likely find that your website visitors are not familiar with library jargon and may not necessarily understand how libraries function. Consider the ways that they labeled categories in the card sorting test and what expectations they have from using other websites. Terms like "Home" and "About" are familiar to users, while other terms such as "Resources" or "Interlibrary Loan" might not be.
5. Design the navigation: With your categories and labels determined, you can begin to design the website navigation. There are various types of navigation, and you'll need to determine which one is the best for organizing your content. Along with the type of navigation, this is also when you'll need to consider things like the placement of the navigation and which pages the navigation will appear on, as well as usage priority of the elements of the menu.
6. Create a wireframe or data model: Once the navigation has been designed, a wireframe, prototype, or data model can be created to share the design

with others. This can done using an Excel spreadsheet, by hand-drawing on a piece of paper, or created with specific prototyping software such as Microsoft Visio. The prototype can be used to get approval from stakeholders or decision-makers and can also be used to perform user testing before translating the design into code.
7. Perform usability testing: Usability testing should be performed before creating the actual website to determine that the navigation is functional and user-friendly. Usability testing at this stage can include user testing, in which you ask representative users to complete several tasks using the navigation, while observing to see where they experience confusion or difficulty. First-click testing can also be useful to quickly determine if users' first click on the website is the one that will lead them toward the content they require. Tree testing can also be used to test the deeper structure of the website, as well as the usefulness of the proposed categories and labels.

NAVIGATION DESIGN

While there are many different flavors of navigational design patterns, navigation designs can be divided into several major categories. Each will require decisions on what will work best for your users and the content on your website.

Flat versus Hierarchical Navigation

- Flat navigation: Used when every page is considered equally important with the same priority in the navigation structure, flat navigation is most common on very small websites. An example of a flat navigation structure is a set of tabs on the website homepage.
- Hierarchical navigation: Used to show information from most important to least important, hierarchical navigation is common on larger sites, including business and e-commerce websites. An example of a hierarchical navigation structure is a retail website where a user can click on 'Books' >> 'Best Sellers' >> 'Fiction.'

Primary versus Secondary Navigation

- Primary navigation: The main navigation on the website, which is featured prominently and links to the most important content. An example of primary navigation is the main top menu on a website.
- Secondary navigation: Supporting navigation that is only included on relevant pages to link to other pages within the same category. An example of secondary navigation that is implemented separately from primary navigation is a website that has the primary navigation menu located

vertically along the left side of the page, and a second menu of secondary (less-important) content located near the bottom of the page.

Global versus Local Navigation

- Global navigation: Navigation that appears on every page of the website. Global navigation allows users to access main pages from anywhere on the site. An example of global navigation is a static menu bar across the top of the page.
- Local navigation: Navigation that shows a user where they are on the website and the content that is nearby. An example of local navigation is bread-crumb navigation, which shows the user the page they are on, plus the next page up in the hierarchy and so on.

Additional Navigation Types

- Single page navigation: Used when all navigation options are on a single page. An example of single page navigation is a simple landing page.
- Contextual navigation: Additional navigation that appears on specific pages. An example of contextual navigation is a link to 'related posts' on a blog post.
- Hidden navigation: Navigation that is hidden until the user takes a specific action in order to save space. An example of hidden navigation is a hamburger menu on a mobile website that the user touches to open up the full menu.

With a variety of different navigational options to choose from, it can be difficult to determine which would work best. Some types of navigation patterns work well for large, e-commerce sites, while other types are better for smaller personal websites or blogs. When it comes to navigation for library websites, research suggests that more library websites are organized in a logical, hierarchical fashion, use primarily horizontal or vertical navigation, include the library's logo in the top center or top-left corner of the page, include contact and location information in the footer or a left sidebar, and include a search option usually in the top right corner.[6] Other research also shows that topic-based navigation is easier for users to navigate than audience-based navigation,[7] meaning navigation that is divided by audience, such as "Undergraduate Students" and "Graduate Students," is generally more difficult for users to navigate.

COMMON NAVIGATION PATTERNS

It wouldn't be possible to designate one navigation pattern as the best option, since there are a large number of different navigation options, many of which can work equally well. Some options are also better suited for certain types of content or designs than others. Table 5.1 contains some of the most common navigation patterns and information about how they are used.

Labels and Terminology

The terminology used in website navigation can greatly affect how user-friendly the website is and is one of the things that can trip up users the most as they attempt to navigate the site. John Kupersmith examined fifty-one usability studies to develop the document "Library Terms That Users Understand."[8] The following terms were the most confusing for library website users, and they should be avoided or, if used, accompanied by explanations of their meaning:

- Acronyms and brand names
- Database
- Library Catalog
- E-journals
- Index
- Interlibrary Loan
- Periodical or Serial
- Reference
- Resource
- Subject categories such as Humanities or Social Sciences[9]

Like in other research, Kupersmith recommends the use of natural language equivalents for top-level navigation and maintaining consistency in the use of terminology across the site. While users may not be familiar with "Interlibrary Loan," they should understand "Borrowing from Other Libraries." Kupersmith found that users most understood terms such as "Find books," "Find articles," and other combinations using natural language and "target words," particularly calls to action like "Get help."

While all libraries and library types will differ somewhat in their use of terminology, developing a list of terms to use on your own website should involve usability testing with your representative users. Card sorting in particular can be used to learn what terms your users prefer and relate to various types of content on your website. In addition to consulting recent research from the professional literature to discover any new determinations on terminology used on library websites, website analytical tools can also be used to capture the terms that users are currently using to search your website for content. Google Analytics and other tools can reveal search terms that are being used by your patrons and help pinpoint content that users are having difficulty finding.

Table 5.1 Common navigation patterns and how they are used.

Navigation Pattern	Usage
Navigation bar	A navigation bar menu can appear at the top or the bottom of a page, with bottom navigation bars popular in mobile applications. Bottom navigation bars are best for menus that only contain three to five items.
Tab menu	Tabs are frequently used for mobile websites and can appear at the top or bottom of the page. Due to limited space, tabs usually feature only the most important content.
Dropdown menu	Dropdown menus include multiple links under an option in a header navigation. Dropdown menus can be difficult for search engines to crawl and can lead to poor accessibility, especially for those using screen readers or keyboard navigation.
Megamenu	Megamenus are an expandable menu that makes the entire navigation visible at once while also conserving space on the page. They are considered more user-friendly than dropdown menus and can accommodate a large number of menu options.
Fixed navigation	Also called "sticky" navigation, fixed navigation is a header menu that stays visible at the top of the screen even as the user scrolls down. This allows the user to navigate to another part of the website without scrolling back up to the top of the page.
Bread crumbs	Bread crumbs show the user where they are in the hierarchy of the website by providing a navigation trail. They can be used in conjunction with another navigation pattern, such as a top navigation bar.
Vertical sidebar	Vertical navigation is most often found on the left side of the page and displays a list of global navigation links that can include primary, secondary, and tertiary levels. It is often useful for single-page applications or for documentation with many topics.
Hamburger menu	The hamburger menu consists of three horizontal lines that can be clicked to open up a full menu. It is often used on mobile websites since it conserves space, but it can also be used to create responsive navigation on desktop sites.
Accordions	Accordion menus use "progressive disclosure" to avoid overwhelming users by showing limited information and allowing the user to open each accordion one at a time to find more details. Accordions are useful in responsive design. Nested accordions can also work well for expert users but may be difficult for novice users.

(Continued)

Table 5.1 (Continued)

Navigation Pattern	Usage
Billboard pattern	Billboard navigation is used on mobile websites and can be used to highlight top tasks. It can appear as a grid, a list of cards, or links that prominently feature the most important content.
Slide-in menus	Slide-in menus contain navigation items that slide in horizontally over the page content to show the menu options for that level. Slide-in menus are often considered to perform poorly as they can be slow and prevent users from quickly jumping to other sections of the navigation.
Curtain navigation	The curtain menu is a type of hidden menu that slides out from the side. They can be fast for jumping to different points in a website and can be used for two or three levels of navigation.
Carousels	Carousels display multiple pieces of content using a slider that rotates across the website. Carousels allow you to prominently feature different content, but they can be poor for accessibility and users have a habit of scrolling past them.
Footer menu	Footer navigation (a type of secondary navigation) usually holds less important links or content such as contact information or social media links and is usually displayed as a bar across the bottom of the page.

BEST PRACTICES

While there are many different options for designing your website navigation, there are some best practices that apply to a majority of situations. Some best practices to keep in mind while designing the website navigation include the following:

- Be consistent: Have a consistent global navigation structure, consistent terminology, consistent placement of links from page to page, consistent styling of links, and consistent ordering of links.
- Use clear language: Labels should be clear and use everyday language. Avoid using library jargon.
- Meet user expectations: Use terminology and link colors consistent with the general web. Put your navigation in a standard location.
- Simplify: Don't use unnecessary icons, or icons that point in multiple directions. Use a simple structure with no unnecessary levels.
- Ensure accessibility: Design your navigation to work for every screen size, including on mobile devices. Provide several ways to access significant

content and make sure important sections are accessible from every page. Make it easy to return to the homepage from any page on the site. Make sure your navigation is accessible to screen readers.
- Be logical: Group information together logically and arrange content in a natural, logical order. Ensure there is a low degree of overlap between categories and sort content according to possible user goals.
- Orient your users: Use bread crumbs to orient users on any page of the site. Any nested navigation should be distinct by using indentation or different type styles. Include a footer.

Mobile Navigation

The navigation used on mobile websites is especially important because users are working within a limited space and may quickly become frustrated by a confusing navigation or menu that is difficult to use. To ensure that the navigation design on a mobile website is useful and accessible, it is sometimes recommended to design for mobile first, with a design that gracefully scales up as different browser sizes are used. The ability to scale according to screen size is known as *responsive design*.

Multiple types of menus are commonly seen on mobile sites. Some of the navigation patterns that are popular for mobile devices include hamburger menus, tab bars, full-page overlays, slide-in menus, nested accordions, and billboard navigation. Navigation menus on mobile sites also frequently use buttons and icons to indicate different types of content. Tab bars tend to work best for websites with only a few navigation options, while hamburger menus can accommodate multiple options but can be less discoverable.

While mobile navigation design can benefit from many of the same best practices that are used in desktop navigation design, the limitations on screen availability also require some additional considerations, such as:

- Avoid using too many icons: In navigation menus such as accordions, icons are often used to indicate the opening and closing of the menu. However, too many icons can cause clutter and pull users' attention in multiple directions.
- Avoid including too many actions: Only include one action at a time to avoid overwhelming users.
- Include an option to go back: This is especially important for navigation patterns that don't allow the user to quickly jump to another section of the website. Users will appreciate an option to go back to the previous page.
- Design for touch: Users on mobile devices are using their fingers to navigate the website menu. Ensure the menu is large enough to accommodate touch.

Tools for IA and Navigation Design

A number of online and digital tools can assist you in creating an information architecture or designing navigation. Some of the most commonly used tools are listed below:

- Treejack

    https://www.optimalworkshop.com/treejack/

    Treejack is a tree testing software offered by Optimal Workshop. Tree testing is a type of usability testing done to evaluate the hierarchy of your design. Optimal Workshop offers a free option that can be used to test up to two tasks, as well as various paid options.
- OptimalSort

    https://www.optimalworkshop.com/optimalsort/

    OptimalSort is also offered by Optimal Workshop and is a card testing software. OptimalSort allows you to perform card testing remotely, potentially reaching more participants. The free plan allows for card sorting with twenty cards, though paid plans offer unlimited cards.
- Microsoft Visio

    https://www.microsoft.com/en-us/microsoft-365/visio/flowchart-software

    Microsoft Visio is a diagramming software offered by Microsoft that can be used to create a prototype for information architecture design. Visio is included as part of Microsoft 365.
- Adobe XD

    https://adobexdplatform.com/

    Adobe XD is software from Adobe that can also be used to design and share information architecture prototypes. Using Adobe XD requires an Adobe license. This option is only available for those who already have the Adobe suite, as the company recently acquired Figma and will eventually sunset XD.
- Figma

    https://www.figma.com/

    Figma is another online software platform that facilitates the design and sharing of prototypes. Figma is free for users with up to three files, though managing unlimited files requires a paid account.

ADDITIONAL RESOURCES

- Cardello, Jen. "The Difference Between Information Architecture (IA) and Navigation." June 22, 2014. https://www.nngroup.com/articles/ia-vs-navigation/.

- Covert, Abby. *How to Make Sense of Any Mess: Information Architecture for Everybody*. Scotts Valley, CA: CreateSpace, 2014.
- Kalbach, James. *Designing Web Navigation: Optimizing the User Experience*. Sebastopol, CA: O'Reilly Media, 2008.
- Rosenfeld, Louis, Peter Morville, and Jorge Arango. *Information Architecture for the World Wide Web: Designing for the Web and Beyond*. Sebastopol, CA: O'Reilly & Associates, 2015.

NOTES

1. Anthony S. Chow, Michelle Bridges, and Patricia Commander, "The Website Design and Usability of US Academic and Public Libraries: Findings from a Nationwide Study," *Reference & User Services Quarterly* 53, no. 3 (2014): 253, http://www.jstor.org/stable/refuseserq.53.3.253.
2. Louis Rosenfeld, Peter Morville, and Jorge Arango, *Information Architecture for the World Wide Web: Designing for the Web and Beyond*. Sebastopol, CA: O'Reilly & Associates, 2015, 233–34.
3. UX Booth Editorial Team, "Complete Beginner's Guide to Information Architecture," *UX Booth*, December 22, 2015, https://uxbooth.com/articles/complete-beginners-guide-to-information-architecture/.
4. Dan Brown, "Eight Principles of Information Architecture," *Bulletin of the American Society for Information Science and Technology* 36, no. 6 (2010): 30, https://doi.org/10.1002/bult.2010.1720360609.
5. Rosenfeld, Morville, and Arango, 4.
6. Chow, Bridges, and Commander, 261.
7. Isabel Vargas Ochoa, "Navigation Design and Library Terminology," *Information Technology and Libraries* 39, no. 4 (2020), https://doi.org/10.6017/ital.v39i4.12123.
8. John Kupersmith, "Library Terms That Users Understand," *UC Berkeley Library: eScholarship* (2012), https://escholarship.org/uc/item/3qq499w7.
9. Kupersmith, 1.

BIBLIOGRAPHY

Brown, Dan. "Eight Principles of Information Architecture." *Bulletin of the American Society for Information Science and Technology* 36, no. 6 (2010): 30–34. https://doi.org/10.1002/bult.2010.1720360609.

Chow, Anthony S., Michelle Bridges, and Patricia Commander. "The Website Design and Usability of US Academic and Public Libraries: Findings from a Nationwide Study." *Reference & User Services Quarterly* 53, no. 3 (2014): 253–65. http://www.jstor.org/stable/refuseserq.53.3.253.

Kupersmith, John. "Library Terms That Users Understand." *UC Berkeley Library: eScholarship* (2012). https://escholarship.org/uc/item/3qq499w7.

Ochoa, Isabel Vargas. "Navigation Design and Library Terminology." *Information Technology and Libraries* 39, no. 4 (2020). https://doi.org/10.6017/ital.v39i4.12123.

Rosenfeld, Louis, Peter Morville and Jorge Arango. *Information Architecture for the World Wide Web: Designing for the Web and Beyond*. Sebastopol, CA: O'Reilly & Associates, 2015.

UX Booth Editorial Team, "Complete Beginner's Guide to Information Architecture," *UX Booth*, December 22, 2015. https://uxbooth.com/articles/complete-beginners-guide-to-information-architecture/.

"Website Navigation Design: Everything You Need to Know." *Trajectory*. Accessed November 16, 2023. https://www.trajectorywebdesign.com/blog/website-navigation-design-guide/.

6

User Experience Design and Usability Testing

Usability testing is essential for good user experience (UX) design and involves real users in the evaluation and testing of website design elements, including the site's navigation and menu labels. Usability testing can and should be done as an iterative process starting before the design of the site, throughout the design process, and continuing after the completion of the site. Usability testing helps designers determine whether users are able to find what they need on the site, carry out necessary tasks, and understand labels, or if they run into navigation issues. Usability testing can help ensure that the website design remains user-centered.

Library staff frequently believe they know how patrons are using their website, but these assumptions can often be wrong. Without the expert knowledge that library staff have acquired through their work, patrons are often unfamiliar with library jargon and terminology and don't always know exactly how libraries work or what services are available to them. Usability testing can help library staff see how patrons are actually using the website and in turn create a website design that allows patrons to find everything they need as easily as possible.

USER EXPERIENCE (UX)

Usability expert Jakob Nielsen has described *user experience* as encompassing "all aspects of the end-user's interaction with the company, its services, and its products."[1] While the website is only one aspect of the patron's total user experience with the library, it is a vital product for ensuring all patrons' needs are met. To provide a great user experience for patrons, the website needs to meet the needs of the patron without causing difficulty for them. Patrons whose only interaction with the library is through the website will form their opinion of the library based primarily on that interaction. "Usable websites increase user satisfaction whereas web sites which violate usability conventions confuse users."[2]

User experience expert Peter Morville describes seven different facets of user experience, which he illustrates with the User Experience Honeycomb.[3] According to the UX honeycomb, a website that offers a good user experience must be useful, usable, desirable, findable, accessible, credible, and valuable. Specifically, the website and its content should fulfill the user's need, be easy to use, use elements of emotional design to evoke appreciation, be easily navigable, be accessible to users with disabilities, evoke the user's trust, and provide value for the organization.

UX RESEARCH

The best way to determine a website's usability is through user research. *User research* is "understanding user behaviors, needs, and motivations through observation techniques, task analysis, and other feedback methodologies."[4]

Figure 6.1 Peter Morville's User Experience Honeycomb. http://semanticstudios.com/user_experience_design/.

The expression "test early, test often," usually applied to software design, is applicable for website design as well. When redesigning an existing website, it can be beneficial to begin by testing the current site design and identifying problems in the design or opportunities for improvement. These findings can then be incorporated into the new website design, which should also be evaluated periodically throughout the design process. Once the new website has launched, additional user testing can determine the overall success of the design and whether any immediate changes are necessary. User testing should be an ongoing process throughout the lifecycle of the website, with the results used to make continuous iterative design improvements. Iteratively evaluating and improving the website design can result in the less-frequent need for a complete website overhaul.

UX research can be either quantitative or qualitative. Quantitative research involves collecting statistical data that can be used as a benchmark or to determine things like how often a user is successful at completing a task on the website or how long they take to complete a common task. Some examples of quantitative research methods include surveys, task analysis using user testing, card sorting, tree testing, first-click testing, and website analytics.

Qualitative research methods are used to collect information about the insights and attitudes of users and includes observations of how users traverse a website with the goal of learning why they behave in a certain way. Examples of qualitative research methods include interviews and focus groups. Researchers can also use a mixed-methods approach to collect both types of data by combining research methods, such as interviewing users before having them perform a task analysis test.

UX research can also be considered either attitudinal or behavioral. *Attitudinal research* measures how users think and feel about the website, as well as their needs and motivations for using it. Examples of attitudinal research include surveys, interviews, and focus groups. *Behavioral research* measures information about how users are actually using the website and what they do when using it. Examples of behavioral research include user testing, A/B testing, and website analytics. It is important to include both types of research methods when performing UX research to glean a full picture of users' interactions with the website, including the what, how, and why of website use.

METHODS OF UX RESEARCH

There are many different methods of gathering user research or performing usability testing, and many of these can be done at low cost or for free. Different methods may be used for testing different things, or during different parts of the design and development process. Some of the most used methods of usability testing are described here.

Surveys

Surveys are a relatively easy way to collect a large amount of data from both current and potential users of the website and gather feedback about the current website or users' needs for the new website. Surveys can be used to gather demographic data about users, as well as information about what they need to accomplish on the website, their overall satisfaction with the site, and what they need that may currently be missing from the site.

Surveys are not a great way to gather information about how users are actually using the site or to assess usability. The way a survey respondent says they use the site in a survey may differ significantly from what they actually do when on the website. The only way to get that information is to observe them using the website, such as during user testing.

When creating a survey, there are several best practices that can ensure you are able to collect the data you need. Some best practices for creating surveys include:

- Keep the survey short.

    Don't try to ask every possible question in one survey. If the survey is too long, users may abandon it partway through, leaving you with incomplete data.
- Choose your questions carefully.

    Will asking for purely demographic information, such as the user's race or age, help you in analyzing their responses? If not, leave those questions out. On the other hand, it may be useful to ask questions about who they are (such as a student or faculty member) in order to group data about different types of users who may have different website needs.
- Create clear and unbiased rating systems.

    If you ask the user to rate something on the website from 1 to 5, make sure you specify that 1 is the lowest and 5 is the highest rating. Otherwise, some users may not interpret the scale the way you intend. Likewise, when creating value ranges, such as very good, good, poor, or very poor, include an equal number of positive and negative options. You can also include a neutral option, though leaving this out will force respondents to choose a side, since neutral answers may or may not provide usable feedback.
- Avoid leading questions.

    Asking a question such as "how easy is the site to use?" includes the term "easy," which may bias respondents to answer in that direction. Instead, make the question neutral by changing the question to a prompt, such as "when navigating the website . . ." with answer options like "I am able to easily find what I need," "I have some trouble but am able to find what I need eventually," and "I am unable to find what I need."
- Make answer options both all-inclusive and mutually exclusive.

When asking questions, make sure the respondent is able to answer by providing all-inclusive answer options. If you ask a question about gender and only provide "male" and "female" as options, non-binary respondents won't be able to provide an answer. Likewise, you want answer options to be mutually exclusive. If you ask respondents to choose an age range, for example, make sure there is no overlap in the options, such as 12-20 years old and 20-40 years old, which would cause confusion for respondents who are twenty years old. When a respondent can respond with multiple answer options, it can negatively impact the data.
- Make most questions optional.

  Most or all of the questions in the survey should be optional, allowing respondents the option to skip a question they don't have an answer for, or one they feel uncomfortable answering. Requiring answers to all questions may cause some users to abandon the survey before finishing or to respond with random answers.
- Don't ask more than one question at one time (double-barreled questions).

  Make sure your questions only ask respondents about one thing. If you ask a question such as "how would you rate the library's collections and services," it forces the respondent to rate both collections and services with the same answer, while they may actually have a different rating for each.
- Use primarily close-ended questions.

  As surveys are primarily used to generate quantitative data, most questions should be close-ended. But it can be useful to include a small number of open-ended questions, or an "other" option with the opportunity for the respondent to fill in an answer. It can also be a good idea to include a broad open-ended question at the end of the survey, such as asking for any additional comments, to allow respondents to provide any feedback that was not addressed in the survey.
- Do a test run of the survey.

  Have a small group of people take the survey before sending it out to everyone to identify any mistakes or problems that need to be corrected.

INTERVIEWS

User interviews can be a great way to learn more about your users, as well as their experiences, challenges, and needs. User interviews are generally conducted before starting the website design, and they are a way to gather more information about your users and how they use your website. Interviews are done with one user at a time and can be conducted in person, by phone, or by online video conference. They are generally around thirty minutes to an hour long. In an interview, you can ask users to rate or rank various website content, as well as ask follow-up questions to gather more in-depth information. Another type of interview format is the contextual interview, in which the researcher watches a user work in their own environment. In contextual interviews, instead of giving the user tasks or prompts, as is done during user testing, the researcher simply watches the user work and concurrently asks questions about what the user is doing and why.

The first step to conducting user interviews is to identify your research goals, or what questions you are trying to answer with the interview. Some example goals may be to find out what patrons like or dislike about the current website, to find out what they need or want that is not currently on the website, or to find out what they find difficult about using the website. Using those goals, you can then formulate your interview questions. Questions should be open-ended and prompt the participant to continue talking. Be sure to avoid invalidating the data by asking the participant any leading questions; instead, questions should be asked in a neutral manner. It's also a good idea to prepare follow-up questions for each original question that you can use to probe further, based on how you anticipate the participant may answer.

Once a set of questions has been created, it is important to do a pilot run of the interview, either with a colleague or with a sample participant. The pilot interview will give you a sense of whether questions could be misunderstood or confusing, whether there are additional questions that should be asked or removed, and to determine a potential order for the questions.

When starting the interview, it can help to get participants to relax and prepare for further discussion by starting off with easy, conversational questions. Asking ice-breaker questions, such as "tell me a little about yourself," can help build a rapport and put the participant at ease.

In interviews, all the information gathered is self-reported by the participant. Self-reported data can sometimes be unreliable if the participant's memory is not accurate, or if they leave out or hold back useful information. While the information gleaned from an interview can still be valuable, only observation or analytics can tell us how they actually use the website. Because of this, interviews are especially helpful when used in combination with other types of usability testing, such as user tests, to learn more about the user and gather insights about their use of the website before doing the test. When using interviews in conjunction with other types of usability testing, it's important to avoid biasing participants by asking them questions during the interview that may lead them to perform the tasks in the other test differently than they might have otherwise.

FOCUS GROUPS

Focus groups are an attitudinal research method used to gather qualitative data about users' emotions, values, beliefs, and mindsets. Like interviews, focus groups are a method that can be more useful before a redesign to collect information about how users feel about the current website. Focus groups usually take around one to two hours and involve a group of five to ten participants. While focus groups are not a good method for testing the usability of a website, they can provide useful information about your patrons' opinions or impressions of the current website.

Focus groups can also be good for understanding your patrons' mental models, as well as for getting a sense of the vocabulary patrons use when discussing various aspects of the website. They can also be more time-efficient than performing individual interviews with the same number of people.

However, focus groups do have certain limitations. As with any self-reported data, focus groups can be prone to user bias or faulty memory. There can also be a negativity bias, which can occur because bad experiences may be more likely to stand out in a user's mind than one in which they encountered no problems. There is also the possibility of priming, in which participants are more likely to discuss certain experiences because another person in the group mentioned it. Additionally, focus groups can be prone to group think, or they may overly emphasize the opinions of the loudest or most talkative members of the group. When conducting a focus group, it's a good idea to offer multiple options for participants to engage with, including both verbal and nonverbal methods, to offset this issue.

Another potential issue is that "users do not always do what they say they will do,"[5] so while focus groups can be useful to gather information about users' concerns or requests, those user requests may not actually provide the best solution to a problem. Visually observing how users engage with the website is the only way to know what users will actually do when using it.

The first step to conducting a focus group is to recruit five to ten participants who are representative of your target audience. You will also want to have an experienced facilitator lead the focus group to obtain the best results. It can be helpful to start the discussion with a low-stakes ice-breaker or warm-up activity that will help participants get into the discussion.

Have a set of questions or prompts planned in advance that will help the facilitator to guide the session. The best questions are relatively broad and open-ended to start, with the facilitator helping the group to focus on more specific areas as the discussion continues. It can be helpful to record these sessions as well as have another observer take notes.

CARD SORTING

Card sorting can be a useful way to determine the best structure for the website either before or early in the design process. It can also help to find the best way to label categories or menu items on the website. Card sorts can be either open or closed. In an open card sort you provide the participant with a set of cards for each page or type of content on the website and have them group the cards together in the way that makes the most sense to them. Then they label each group in the way they feel best describes that content. Some examples of possible cards include:

- Interlibrary Loan
- Getting Help
- Mission & Vision Statements
- Staff Contact Information
- Scheduling a Consultation
- Circulation Policies

In a closed card sort, you provide predefined categories and have participants sort the cards into those categories. It can be useful to do a combination of open and closed card sorting, first doing an open card sort to determine labels for each grouping, followed by a closed card sort to determine how well the content falls under those labels.

Card sorting can be done individually or in groups. Individual card sorting sessions may allow the facilitator to ask additional questions as the participant sorts the cards, while having a group work collaboratively can speed up the process and provide a group consensus on the content organization.

Card sorting can be done as a remote test or in person. During in person card sorting tests, index cards or Post-it Notes can be used to allow the participant to physically sort the cards. Remote tests can be done using specialized card sorting software that allows you to gather data from more participants, including those in different locations. Card sorting software will also automatically analyze the data, allowing for quicker conclusions. On the other hand, with remote testing the facilitator is not able to ask questions about why the participant made certain decisions or see the process they go through to arrive at the final sort. Some options for performing remote card sorting tests include OptimalSort (Optimal Workshop), UserZoom, and Maze.

When performing card sorting tests, it's a best practice to limit the number of cards per test to avoid overwhelming the participant. Usually, thirty to forty cards are the maximum recommended to use at one time. For larger, more complex websites, multiple card sorts may need to be performed for various groupings of content. It is also a good idea to randomize the order of the cards for each participant to avoid any bias caused by the placement of the cards.

TREE TESTING

While card sorting can help you decide how to group content together on a website and what labels to use, tree testing can be used as a follow-up method to test the resulting navigation structure and see if it actually works in practice.

In a tree test, the hierarchical structure of the website is evaluated by having participants locate specific resources using the site hierarchy. Like card sorting, tree testing can be done before any actual design or layout work on the website is completed. Tree testing can be done with paper, or by creating a clickable, accordian-type online menu for users to click through, but there are also online software options, such as UserZoom and Treejack (Optimal Workshop), that can make gathering and analyzing the data much faster and easier.

Tree testing can use the same types of prompts as in user testing, by asking users to find specific pages or resources using the website navigation. When formulating prompts, keep them short and simple so that users aren't distracted by too many potential keywords, and also to avoid using the name of the label within the question and leading users to the answer.

Some examples of prompts for tree testing might include:

- You would like to borrow a book that the library doesn't have. Where do you go to find information on how to obtain the book?
- You are doing research for a school project and having trouble finding relevant resources. Where would you click to get research assistance?
- You would like a librarian to provide an orientation session for your students. Where would you go to make this request?

Tree testing can be either qualitative or quantitative. In quantitative tree testing, a large sample size can be used to gather data about how long users take to locate a resource, what percentage of users are able to locate a resource, or the most frequent paths taken to find a resource. One downside of quantitative tree testing is that you aren't able to ask follow-up questions or gather information on why users chose a particular path.

Qualitative tree testing allows for this type of interaction; however, it is not the best way to gather statistical data. A good approach would be to perform a small qualitative tree test up front to pilot the test and ensure that participants understand the tasks, as well as to get information about why users chose certain paths, to determine which labels were confusing to users, and to gain feedback on improving these issues. Once those insights are gathered, a quantitative tree test can be performed to gather a larger amount of data on which navigational options work the best.

WIREFRAMING/PROTOTYPING

Prototypes are usability testing methods that can be used early in the design process to test things like layout and structural elements of a website, or that can be used toward the end of the design process for more full-featured usability testing. Prototypes can be low fidelity, such as a simple wireframe drawing, or they can be medium or high fidelity. Prototypes can contain content and images and can be static or responsive. They can be used to visualize a design, explore technical feasibility, or test the effectiveness of a particular design option.

Low-fidelity prototypes are quick to develop and easy to use, and they can be effective for testing early in the design process. A medium-fidelity prototype may be more effective further into the design process, when presenting a more complete design to others for feedback. High-fidelity prototypes can be detailed replicas of how the site will look, but without the full functionality of a live site. They can be used for usability testing to determine how users interact with the site and how they feel about the overall visuals of the site.

Low-fidelity prototypes can be made using a paper sketch to quickly test design ideas. The idea is to test potential layouts, information architecture, content areas, structure, task flows, and interaction design in an environment where changes can be made quickly and then retested. This results in rapid iteration of design ideas in an easy and inexpensive manner.

Wireframes are a type of prototype that are a simplified representation of the site design and can include lines, text, and structural elements, but they usually don't include visual design elements or color. Wireframes can be hand drawn or electronic using various prototyping software, such as Adobe XD, Figma, Sketch, and Framer. Of these options, Figma and Framer both offer free versions of the software.

FIRST CLICK TESTING

Wireframes or prototypes can also be used in first click testing, where a participant is asked to complete a specific task while researchers note where they go first. This type of testing can help you to evaluate the navigation and structure of the website, as well as the language used for labels and links, the placement of buttons or menus, and what content is prioritized on the homepage. Research has shown that 87 percent of users will succeed in completing their task if their first click is correct, whereas only 46 percent will eventually succeed if they navigate down the wrong path.[6]

First click testing should begin with the creation of a set of prompts that represent common tasks a user might need to do on the website, such as finding a known item or scheduling a consultation. The correct path for completing each task should be documented ahead of time in order to easily take notes on whether or not the participant is successful.

Each task should be started from the homepage of the website to avoid complicating the navigation from subsequent pages within the site. In addition to tracking the participant's clicks, the amount of time it takes them to choose a first click should also be documented. Longer times can indicate a confusing navigation that may need to be refined. Participants should not be told they are participating in a first click test, as this may cause them to behave differently than they otherwise might have. However, after the test, the participant should fill out a satisfaction rating or confidence scale on whether or not they felt they were able to find the correct information.

PREFERENCE TESTING

Preference testing is another research method that can also be used in conjunction with wireframes or prototypes in the early stages of the design process to test out early designs before committing them to code. Preference testing can help you refine the design of a website based on user preference instead of guesswork. It is also simple, inexpensive, and easy to conduct.

When doing preference testing, it's a good idea to limit design variations to two or three designs to avoid overwhelming the participant with too many choices. Preference testing can determine which design users prefer and why, as well as their perception or emotional response to the design or the perceived trustworthiness of the website.

Preference tests can also be either qualitative or quantitative. In qualitative preference testing, the participant is shown the design variants and asked about which one they prefer, why, and their overall impressions of the design. Quantitative preference testing generally involves using a survey where participants can select the design they prefer from a set of options. This form of preference testing allows the researcher to gather data from a larger number of participants, but it doesn't allow for the follow-up questioning that qualitative testing does.

Preference testing does have limitations, including a potential difficulty in gathering information about why a certain design is preferable if participants are not able to explain exactly why they prefer one design over another. And while preference testing can help determine users' preferences for a particular design, it does not test the usability or functionality of the actual site.

Usually around twenty to thirty participants are needed in preference testing to allow for a large enough sample size. As in other types of testing, recruiting a representative sample of users is important. Each participant can be shown two or three variations of a design and asked to choose which they prefer. Options for gathering additional information during preference testing include:

- Asking open-ended questions (why is the design preferred? how easy is it to navigate?)
- Choosing from a closed list of adjectives (offer the participant three to five words to choose from to describe the design)
- Coming up with their own adjectives (have participants come up with three to five words to describe the design)
- Numerically rate designs (have participants rate certain elements on a scale, i.e., 1-10)

USER TESTING

User testing is one of the easiest and more practical methods of usability testing and one of the best ways to determine how user-friendly a website design actually is. During user testing, participants are asked to respond to a set of prompts while their actions are observed and notes are taken on how they complete each task. The goal of user testing is to determine whether users are able to easily complete common tasks on the website and to locate areas of the site where users run into problems or display confusion.

Steve Krug, who wrote the seminal text on web usability—*Don't Make Me Think: A Common Sense Approach to Web Usability*—also wrote a follow-up book on how to easily perform usability testing, entitled *Rocket Surgery Made Easy*. Krug recommends testing just three users because "the first three users are very likely to encounter many of the most significant problems related to the tasks you're testing."[7] Jakob Nielsen suggests testing five users.[8] He also recommends performing multiple tests whenever possible, including different sets of tests for different types of users (i.e., faculty, undergraduates, and graduate students; or teens, adults, and children).

Usability testing doesn't need to be formal, expensive, or time-consuming to be effective. It can also be done in person, remotely through web conferencing software, or with a hybrid approach, where the participant is in one room and a video feed of the test is routed to observers in another room. Morae, a paid software that was created to assist with usability testing, can be used to record, analyze, edit, and share test sessions. If the sessions are to be recorded, it may be advisable to create a consent form and have the participants sign it before beginning the test. The low-cost or free option of user testing only requires a computer with internet access, a participant, and an observer to take notes. It can help to have two people work together to perform the sessions—one to go through the prompts and the other to take notes.

Rocket Surgery Made Easy describes in detail how to perform user testing in an easy and simple way. The basic steps for performing a user test are as follows:

1. Determine what questions you want the test to answer, for example:
   - Do users understand the terminology used on the website?
   - Are users able to find a known item using the website?
   - Can users find where to get help if they need assistance?
2. Recruit and schedule participants:
   - Decide how many users you will test, and schedule slightly more than that number to account for no-shows.
   - Consider offering incentives for participation, such as gift cards or library swag.

3. Create a set of prompts (enough for an approximately thirty-minute session) for users to perform that will answer the questions from step one, for example:
   - Use the website to find out what time the library opens on Sundays.
   - Locate the call number for *The Grapes of Wrath* using the website.
4. Write a script for the sessions that:
   - Explains the purpose of the test and reassures the participant that it is the website that is being tested, not them.
   - Describes how the test will work.
   - Reminds the participant to talk through their process out loud.
5. Conduct the sessions:
   - Give the participant each prompt and either record their actions or take detailed notes about how they complete the task.
   - Do not interfere or give the user hints; if they fail to complete the task, it provides valuable insight about the website design.
   - Record what the user does, where they have trouble, whether they are able to complete the task, and how quickly they do so.
6. Analyze the results of the sessions to determine what elements of the site need to be adjusted.
7. Make changes to the design based on the analysis.
8. Repeat user testing with the new website design.

While user testing can be performed using early versions of the website design, it also can easily be used to gather ongoing feedback after the site launches. Regular user testing can lead to continuous, incremental improvement of the site and over time, a better experience for users.

ONLINE UX TOOLS

- Crazy Egg
    https://www.crazyegg.com/
    Crazy Egg is an analytics platform that tracks user behavior. Along with heatmapping, Crazy Egg also offers recordings, surveys, error tracking, A/B testing, and traffic analysis. Crazy Egg offers a thirty-day free trial and several monthly paid options.
- Hotjar
    https://www.hotjar.com/
    Hotjar is an online platform that can track how users interact with your website using heatmaps, recordings of users using the website, surveys, and interviews. Each product has a free option including thirty-five daily heatmapping sessions, three surveys with up to twenty responses per month, and up to five thirty-minute interviews per month.

- Maze
    https://maze.co/
    Maze is an online usability testing tool that offers the ability to conduct surveys, interviews, card sorting, tree testing, and prototype testing. Maze provides a free option that allows for one study per month, or several paid options.
- Optimal Workshop
    https://www.optimalworkshop.com/
    Optimal Workshop is a user-experience research platform with several products that can help you gather and analyze data using remote testing methods. Products include options for card sorting, tree testing, first click testing, online surveys, and qualitative research analysis. There is a free option that includes limited use of each of the products, as well as paid plans for unlimited use.
- Optimizely
    https://www.optimizely.com/
    Optimizely calls itself a digital experience platform that offers A/B testing, multivariate testing, and analytics tracking. Optimizely also integrates with Google Analytics and Microsoft 365. While there is no free option, you can request a demo; and you must request customized pricing information.
- UserZoom
    https://www.userzoom.com/
    UserZoom is another online platform that allows users to conduct tests including interviews, user testing, card sorting, tree testing, and clickstream tracking via heatmaps. There is not a free option; however, they do offer a free trial of the platform, as well as discounts for both universities and nonprofits.

ADDITIONAL RESOURCES

The following books, articles, and websites provide more detailed information and further study on some of the topics discussed in this chapter.

- Blakiston, Rebecca. *Usability Testing*. Lanham: Rowman & Littlefield, 2014.
- Dobbs, Aaron W. *The Library Assessment Cookbook*. Chicago: Association of College and Research Libraries, 2017.
- Krug, Steve. *Don't Make Me Think*. Berkeley, CA: New Riders, 2019.
- Krug, Steve. *Rocket Surgery Made Easy: The Do-It-Yourself Guide to Finding and Fixing Usability Problems*. Berkeley, CA: New Riders, 2010.

- Michigan Publishing. *Weave: Journal of Library User Experience*. https://journals.publishing.umich.edu/weaveux/.
- Nielsen Norman Group. NN/g Nielsen Norman Group. https://www.nngroup.com/.
- Schmidt, Aaron, and Amanda Etches. *Useful Usable Desirable: Applying User Experience Design to Your Library*. Chicago: ALA Editions, 2014.
- U.S. General Services Administration. Usability.gov. https://www.usability.gov/index.html.

NOTES

1. Don Norman and Jakob Nielsen, "The Definition of User Experience (UX)," accessed September 29, 2023, https://www.nngroup.com/articles/definition-user-experience/.
2. Thomas Churm, "An Introduction to Website Usability Testing," accessed September 29, 2023, https://usabilitygeek.com/an-introduction-to-website-usability-testing/.
3. Peter Morville, "User Experience Design," June 24, 2004, http://semanticstudios.com/user_experience_design/.
4. "User Research Basics," Usability.gov, accessed September 29, 2023, https://www.usability.gov/what-and-why/user-research.html.
5. Therese Fessenden, "Focus Groups 101," July 31, 2022, https://www.nngroup.com/articles/focus-groups-definition/.
6. Jeff Sauro, "Getting the First Click Right," October 19, 2011, https://measuringu.com/first-click/.
7. Steve Krug, *Rocket Surgery Made Easy: The Do-It-Yourself Guide to Finding and Fixing Usability Problems* (Berkeley, CA: New Riders Publishing, 2010), 43.
8. Jakob Nielsen, "Why You Only Need to Test with 5 Users," March 18, 2000, https://www.nngroup.com/articles/why-you-only-need-to-test-with-5-users/.

BIBLIOGRAPHY

Churm, Thomas. "An Introduction to Website Usability Testing." Accessed September 29, 2023. https://usabilitygeek.com/an-introduction-to-website-usability-testing/.

Fessenden, Therese. "Focus Groups 101." July 31, 2022. https://www.nngroup.com/articles/focus-groups-definition/.

Krug, Steve. *Rocket Surgery Made Easy: The Do-It-Yourself Guide to Finding and Fixing Usability Problems*. Berkeley, CA: New Riders Publishing, 2010.

Morville, Peter. "User Experience Design." June 24, 2004. http://semanticstudios.com/user_experience_design/.

Nielsen, Jakob. "Why You Only Need to Test with 5 Users." March 18, 2000. https://www.nngroup.com/articles/why-you-only-need-to-test-with-5-users/.

Norman, Don, and Jakob Nielsen. "The Definition of User Experience (UX)." Accessed September 29, 2023. https://www.nngroup.com/articles/definition-user-experience/.

Sauro, Jeff. "Getting the First Click Right." October 19, 2011. https://measuringu.com/first-click/.

"User Research Basics." Usability.gov. Accessed September 29, 2023. https://www.usability.gov/what-and-why/user-research.html.

7

Accessibility and Universal Design

The Centers for Disease Control and Prevention estimates that as many as one in four adults in the United States have some type of disability.[1] These disabilities can be auditory, cognitive, neurological, physical, speech, visual, or some combination of these. Website accessibility is the concept of ensuring that your website can be used by anyone, regardless of ability. Website accessibility is a legal requirement for many libraries, as well as a web design best practice. Along with the principles of universal design, following accessibility guidelines will make your website more functional and easier for all of your patrons to use.

Government websites, as well as universities that receive federal dollars, are subject to accessibility legislation, including the Americans with Disabilities Act (ADA) and Section 508 of the Rehabilitation Act of 1973. The Americans with Disabilities Act is a U.S. civil rights law enacted in 1990 that applies to any business in the private or public sector and prevents discrimination on the basis of disability. The ADA prohibits discrimination in "places of public accommodations," which is understood to include digital and web content.

Section 508 applies to federal agencies and mandates that all information and communications technology is accessible to those with disabilities, including websites, software, electronic documents, and multimedia content. Noncompliance with Section 508 requirements can result in the loss of federal funding, while noncompliance with the ADA can result in lawsuits, with 2,387 such lawsuits filed in 2022.[2] However, even with these potential legal ramifications, Utah State University's Web AIM Million Project reported in 2023 that over 96 percent of the top one million homepages were not compliant with accessibility requirements, with an average of fifty accessibility issues per homepage.[3]

In addition to making your website accessible for legal and ethical reasons, website accessibility can also benefit users without disabilities. People using mobile devices, older adults, people with temporary physical disabilities (such as a broken arm), people accessing the website in bright sunlight or in a noisy environment, or those using outdated technology or who have limited bandwidth can all benefit from accessible website design.[4] In fact, "case studies show that accessible websites have better search results, reduced maintenance costs, and increased audience reach, among other benefits."[5]

With website accessibility being so important and having the potential to impact so many of your users, accessible website design should be at the forefront when planning a new or updated website. There are numerous tools available that can help with identifying accessibility issues in a current website design, as well as providing recommendations for fixing and improving accessibility issues. However, it takes specialized knowledge and skills to properly test a website for compliance with accessibility guidelines. If those skills are not available in-house, it may be advisable to hire a professional consultant to ensure your website meets all the legal requirements for accessibility.

ASSISTIVE TECHNOLOGY

Several types of assistive technology devices are available today that your patrons may currently be using to access content on your website. It is important to be aware of the various types of devices that are commonly used and consider these when designing your website. The main types of assistive technology devices include:

- Screen Readers
    Screen reading technology allows those who are blind or who have visual impairments to access the content of digital resources by using software that reads the text of web content aloud. Some popular screen readers include JAWS, NVDA, Apple VoiceOver, and Chrome Vox.
- Screen Magnifiers
    Magnifying technology is used by those with visual impairments who need text to be in a larger size in order to read. Some magnifiers may be combined with screen reading software as well. Some examples of screen magnifiers include SuperNova, ZoomText, and MagniSight.
- Literacy Software
    Literacy software can be helpful for users who have cognitive issues, such as learning disabilities, or difficulty with reading or writing. Such software can provide dictionaries, translators, highlighting functions, or the ability to scan and play back passages of text. Some examples of literacy software include Read&Write GOLD, Kurzweil 1000 and 3000, and WYNN Wizard.
- Speech Recognition Software

Speech recognition software allows users to provide verbal input to create written documents, or to navigate website content. Some examples of speech recognition software include Nuance Dragon Professional, Apple Voice Control, and Windows Voice Recognition.
- Peripheral Devices
Peripheral devices include headsets, speakers, microphones, touchpads, and keyboards and are all adaptive devices that can assist users with accessing online content.

WEB CONTENT ACCESSIBILITY GUIDELINES (WCAG)

The Web Content Accessibility Guidelines (known as WCAG), published by the Web Accessibility Initiative of the World Wide Web Consortium (the W3C), are considered the working standard for digital accessibility. While adherence to WCAG guidelines is not yet legally required, WCAG covers all the criteria required by Section 508, as well as the recommendations outlined by the ADA. WCAG was recently updated from version 2.1 to version 2.2 as of October 2023. Version 3.0 is currently in draft, though it's unlikely to be complete for some time. The WCAG guidelines are cumulative and WCAG versions 2.0 and 2.1 are still considered recommended by the W3C. Version 2.2 extends the previous version with an additional nine success criteria, and the W3C recommends using this version to maximize accessibility. WCAG is also considered an international standard for web accessibility, with WCAG 2.0 also being an ISO standard (ISO/IEC 40500).

WCAG Conformance Levels

WCAG has three levels of conformance: Level A, Level AA, and Level AAA. Level A is the lowest level of conformance and the least strict. Level A should be considered the bare minimum for meeting accessibility standards and is the initial level to aim for if your current website has never been aligned to WCAG guidelines. Websites that don't conform with Level A are likely to have serious accessibility issues and may be unusable for those with certain disabilities.

Level AA is the mid-level for accessibility conformance and is generally considered the best practice for most websites to conform to. The conformance levels are cumulative, and a website that is conformant with Level AA is also conformant with all of the success criteria for Level A and is likely to be accessible for a majority of users.

Level AAA is the highest level of conformance but is not considered the best practice because it is not yet possible for certain types of content to conform to every WCAG guideline. The W3C also notes that "even content that conforms to the highest level (AAA) will not be accessible to individuals with all types, degrees, or combinations of disability."[6] Level AAA conformance requires that a website conform to every guideline in WCAG, which in version 2.2 consists of eighty-six individual success criteria.

While WCAG Level AA conformance is considered the best practice and many online accessibility evaluation tools assess websites against these standards, "automated tools can only detect ~30% of WCAG issues."[7] To ensure conformance to accessibility guidelines and meet legal accessibility requirements, a combination of automated testing, manual testing, and testing using assistive technology, such as screen readers, is the only truly thorough approach.

The Four Principles of Accessibility

The success criteria laid out in the WCAG guidelines have been created to follow four principles of accessibility.[8] To ensure users can adequately access and use a website, the website must be:

1. Perceivable

    For website users to be able to effectively use the website, they must be able to perceive the content. This applies to both the information and the user interface components on the website. For a blind or low-vision user, the content and user interface must be perceivable through assistive technology such as screen reader software in order to be accessible.
2. Operable

    An accessible website must be operable for all users, which means they must be able to interact with the website in every way necessary. This can include site navigation, menu links, and audio and video content. Keeping a website simple can make it more easily operable for users with disabilities.
3. Understandable

    Web content must also be understandable for all users. This can be especially important for users with cognitive disabilities or those who speak other languages than the one used on your website. Ensuring

Table 7.1 Number of success criteria for each WCAG conformance level.

Conformance Level	# of Success Criteria
Level A	32 success criteria
Level AA	23 success criteria (+ 32 Level A criteria = 55)
Level AAA	31 success criteria (+ 32 Level A criteria + 23 Level AA criteria = 86)

content is understandable can include using clear, simple language, an intuitive organizational structure, and easily identifiable navigation.
4. Robust

For website content to be robust, it must be able to be easily interpreted by all users, including those using assistive technology. Using well-structured HTML, including semantic elements such as <form> and <table> along with structural elements such as headings, can make your content easier to parse for screen readers and other assistive technologies.

Avoiding Common Accessibility Errors

While a thorough accessibility audit is the only way to ensure your website conforms to WCAG accessibility guidelines, some accessibility issues are considered very common, and knowing what they are can help you avoid creating them during the design process and prevent the need to rectify them later.

Table 7.2 includes some of the most common website accessibility errors and how to address them to conform with WCAG guidelines.

ACCESSIBLE RICH INTERNET APPLICATIONS STANDARD (WAI-ARIA)

Although keeping websites simple and using semantic markup such as that found in HTML5 can make websites more accessible, many modern websites feature dynamic content that can provide its own barriers to accessibility. Dynamic content is content that changes in some way in response to user interactivity. Some technologies that are often used in creating dynamic content include CSS, JavaScript, DOM, and AJAX. The use of these types of technologies results in something called rich internet applications (RIA), which can include features such as dialogs, tooltips, drop-down menus, date pickers, and drag and drop controls.

To ensure that rich internet applications are also accessible for all users, the W3C created the Accessible Rich Internet Applications standard (WAI-ARIA). The current version of WAI-ARIA is version 1.2, which was recommended in June 2023, while version 1.3 is currently under development.

WAI-ARIA defines a set of attributes—including roles, states, and properties—that should be included in the code of RIAs to make them accessible. Both states and properties provide specific information about an element, but state expresses a characteristic of an object that is subject to change due to a user action or automated process, while property represents a value or essential attribute of an object. States and properties are both frequently referred to as "attributes" by the WAI-ARIA specification.

Roles indicate the type of element and include semantic information about the element's behavior that allow assistive technologies or browsers to

Table 7.2 Common accessibility issues and how to address them.

Accessibility Issue	WCAG Guideline/ Level	How to Address
Images missing alternative text	WCAG 1.1.1, A	Include "alt text" for all images so that visually impaired users will be able to access the content conveyed by the image.
Untitled multimedia content	WCAG 1.1.1, A	Use a title tag with a description that conveys the purpose or content of the video so that visually impaired users will know what the video is about.
Using color to convey information	WCAG 1.4.1, A	Don't only use color cues to convey information, as visually impaired users or users with color blindness will not be able to perceive it. Instead include text in addition to color.
Insufficient color contrast	WCAG 1.4.3, AA	Ensure text has a contrast ratio of at least 4.5:1 so that it is perceivable for users with low vision or color blindness.
Using images as text	WCAG 1.4.5 (images of text), AA	Avoid using images of text in place of actual text as it will not be accessible to visually impaired users. You can also use "alt text" to convey all of the text from the image if necessary.
Videos without captions	WCAG 1.2.3 (prerecorded), A WCAG 1.2.4 (live), AA	Include captions for all videos so that hearing impaired users will have access to the information.
Inaccessible forms	WCAG 1.3.5 (input purpose), AA WCAG 3.3.1 (error identification), A	Include labels, clear instructions, error indicators, and keyboard navigation to make it possible for visually impaired users or those using keyboard navigation to access and submit a form.

(Continued)

Table 7.2 (Continued)

Accessibility Issue	WCAG Guideline/ Level	How to Address
Lack of keyboard navigation	WCAG 2.1.1, A	Ensure every interactive element on a page can be selected using the tab key so that users unable to use a mouse can access it. Also include a "skip to results" or "skip to main content" link at the top of the page so that users with screen readers don't have to listen to the entire page before getting to the content they need.
Non-descriptive links	WCAG 2.4.4, A	Use descriptive text to describe links such as "New Books List" rather than "Click Here," so that when a screen reader reads the link text the user will know where the link is taking them. Also use alt text when using images or icons as links, and use ARIA labels to describe menus, especially the "tabpanel," "tab," and "tablist" roles.
Poor site structure	WCAG 2.4.6 (headings), AA WCAG 3.2.3 (navigation), AA	Structure the website using hierarchical headings and present information in a logical order, so that visually impaired users are able to easily browse through the site. Use consistent navigation across the website to help orient users.
Empty headings	WCAG 2.4.6, AA	Ensure all headings have relevant text so that users using screen readers will be able to browse through the headings to get relevant information.

Accessibility and Universal Design

provide this information to the user. HTML5 includes semantic elements that don't require the use of ARIA roles; however, roles are needed if using non-semantic elements such as <div> and <span> tags so that assistive devices can recognize what that element is being used for.

Roles can be categorized as:

- Abstract roles: These define abstract concepts of taxonomy and are usually not needed.
- Widget roles: These define user interface components, such as menu items, progress bars, and tab lists.
- Document structure roles: These define structures of the web page.
- Landmark roles: These define significant regions of a page, such as main, navigation, and search.
- Live region roles: These define areas such as a chat widget or weather widget, where the content is periodically updated automatically.
- Window roles: These define structures that are windows within the browser, such as dialog boxes.

Some of the more common attributes (states and properties) and roles that often need to be used include:

- aria-checked = "true" or "false"
- aria-current = "true" or "false"
- aria-describedby = "date-format"
- aria-expanded = "true" or "false"
- aria-hidden = "true" or "false"
- aria-required = "true" or "false"
- role = "banner"
- role = "search"
- role = "tablist"

The WAI-ARIA specification also requires mandatory focus navigation, which provides alternate keyboard interactions for users who are not able to use pointer devices such as a mouse, trackpad, or touchscreen. When using <div> or <span> tags for interactive elements, focus management will require using tabindex= "0" to focus the keyboard on the element, an event listener if the element accepts keyboard input, and an ARIA role to allow a screen reader to identify the element.

Common ARIA Errors to Avoid

WAI-ARIA is less understood generally than the WCAG guidelines, and it can be easy to apply the standards incorrectly. One thing to keep in mind

Table 7.3   Common ARIA errors.

Common ARIA Error	Explanation
Incorrect syntax	• Role values must be lowercase. • Check for correct spelling or spacing of roles or attributes. • Make sure to use the correct ARIA attribute for the role.
Creating your own role or attribute	• The roles and attributes that you use must be in the WAI-ARIA specifications. • Creating your own role or attributes will result in assistive devices not being able to interpret the content.
Children roles without parents/Parent roles without children	• Certain roles cannot be used without the related parent/child role. • For example, the child role "tab" must be accompanied by its parent role—"tablist." • The parent role "menu" must be followed by its "menu item" children.
Invalid ID references	• Attribute ID references must refer to an ID that exists within the document.
Missing required attributes	• Certain roles require specific attributes and cannot be properly used without them. • For example, the "slider" role must include attributes for "aria-valuemin," "aria-valuemax," and "aria-valuenow."

is that ARIA should not be used unless it's necessary. HTML5 already includes accessible elements and is the preferred method when available. Using ARIA when there is a valid HTML5 element that could be used instead can cause the element to become inaccessible—the direct opposite of the goal. ARIA labels should only be used when there is not a valid HTML5 element available.

Table 7.3 includes some of the most common errors made when using ARIA. These errors can cause screen readers to misinterpret or be unable to convey the necessary information to the user.

UNIVERSAL DESIGN

Universal design has been defined as "the design and composition of an environment so that it can be accessed, understood and used to the greatest extent possible by all people regardless of their age, size, ability or disability."[9] While most products are designed to be usable for the average person, universal design encourages the design of products that are usable for everyone, without the need for specialized adaptations.

Universal design can be applied to nearly everything, including streets and sidewalks, doors, information and communications technology, and in teaching and learning. Universal design can also be applied to website design, to create websites that are usable for all.

Websites created with universal design in mind will be more accessible to users with a wide variety or combination of disabilities, including:

- Blindness
- Low vision
- Color blindness
- Deafness
- Hearing loss
- Speech disabilities
- Learning disabilities
- Cognitive disabilities
- Neurological disabilities
- Physical disabilities

However, similar to accessibility, universal design can also provide usability benefits to users without disabilities as well. All users, regardless of ability, can benefit from universal design because it emphasizes:

- Meeting the needs of all users
- Minimizing the need for assistive technology
- User-friendly design
- Social inclusion, diversity, and equity
- Promoting independence

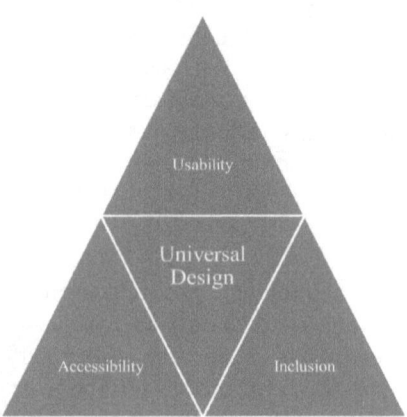

Figure 7.1 Universal design and its relationship to usability, accessibility, and inclusion. Brighid M. Gonzales.

The 7 Principles of Universal Design

The concept of universal design is based on seven principles, known as "The 7 Principles of Universal Design," which were developed by a group at the Center for Universal Design at North Carolina State University in 1997.[10] These principles guide the design of products toward universal design, and they can be applied to all products and environments, including websites. The 7 Principles of Universal Design include:

1. Equitable Use
   The design should be useful to people with diverse abilities. It should provide the same means of use, avoid stigmatizing users, equally provide provisions for privacy and security, and appeal to all users. An example of this principle is a website that can be used by everyone, including blind users.
2. Flexibility in Use
   The design should accommodate a range of abilities and preferences, such as a choice in methods, right- or left-handed access, and adaptability to the user's pace. An example of flexibility in website design is offering a choice of watching a video, reading captions, or listening to the audio of multimedia content.
3. Simple and Intuitive Use
   The design should be easy for all users to understand regardless of their experience, knowledge, or language skills. The design should not be unnecessarily complex and should align with users' expectations. An example of intuitiveness in a website is having the organization's logo in the top left of the website and linking the logo back to the site's homepage, a website convention users have come to expect.
4. Perceptible Information
   The design should communicate information to the user effectively regardless of the user's abilities. This includes using different formats to present information, ensuring adequate color contrast, and being compatible with assistive devices. A website that includes both images and text that convey the same essential information is an example of this principle.
5. Tolerance for Error
   The design should be tolerant of user error, including providing warnings and fail-safe features. An example of tolerating errors is the inclusion of descriptive error messages when a user enters the wrong information into a form so that they know what they did wrong and what they need to enter instead.
6. Low Physical Effort
   The design should be efficient and not cause fatigue in the user, such as by minimizing repetitive actions. For website design, an example of low

physical effort could be including keyboard shortcuts so that users with screen readers can skip directly to the content they need.
7. Size and Space for Approach and Use
The design should provide appropriate size and space regardless of the user's body or mobility. In website design, an example of this principle is creating your website so that it is easy to use on mobile devices as well as on desktop browsers.

Applying Universal Design to Website Design

Universal design is related to accessibility in many ways, and many of the methods for applying universal design to a website overlap with the guidelines for creating accessible websites. The 7 Principles of Universal Design also overlap with the Four Principles of Accessibility (perceivable, operable, understandable, and robust). Using both sets of principles to inform your website's design can ultimately make your site much more inclusive of all users.

However, there are some important distinctions between accessibility and universal design. Accessibility involves using methods for ensuring your website is accessible to users with a variety of potential disabilities, whereas universal design is about designing a website that is accessible to all users regardless of ability, situation, or environment. For example, while universal design principles take disabilities into consideration, they also ensure usability for non-disabled users. This can involve things like ensuring text is readable even if the user is outside on a bright day, touch controls on a mobile site that can accommodate larger-size fingers, text that is simple enough to understand even if it is in a user's secondary language, and ensuring content is still navigable if images on the website fail to load. In addition to physical disabilities, universal design also considers cognitive disabilities, such as learning disabilities, neurodiversity, and intellectual disabilities.

As with implementing accessibility methods, it is important to thoroughly test a website to ensure that universal design elements work as intended. Universal design takes all users into account, including those accessing the website in varying environments and situations that may differ from the environment in which the site was created. To account for these differences, it is important to test the website on multiple browsers, at various network speeds, and using various assistive technologies. Creating user personas can also help to ensure that your website takes a variety of user types into consideration during the design process. If it's possible, involving users with disabilities during the design process can also be helpful.

There are a number of ways that universal design can be applied to the design and development of websites, including:

Structure and Design

- Reduce visual clutter ("Progressive Disclosure" is the process of displaying only the most important information on the screen and allowing the user to drill down for more information as needed, reducing visual clutter).
- Design with mobile accessibility in mind.
- Create a logical page structure using headings.
- Be consistent about the placement of logos, menus, and other elements that recur across multiple pages of the site.
- Use semantic HTML elements such as <legend>, <label>, and <caption> to allow users with screen readers to browse by content type.
- Use bread crumbs and headings to orient the user on the site.
- Avoid using too many different colors or fonts to prevent sensory overload.
- Use an easy-to-follow writing style and avoid using unnecessary jargon.
- Avoid using blocks of text. Instead use bullet points and keep paragraphs short and concise.
- Include keyboard shortcuts.

Text Font, Size, and Color

- Use strong color contrast for text.
- Use true text that allows users to resize the font as needed without distorting the page layout rather than using images of text that can't be resized.
- Use standardized sans-serif fonts in adequate sizes (ideally nothing below a 10-point font).
- Use "em" or "rem" CSS styles for fonts to accommodate users who need to resize font or change font style for readability.
- Avoid underlining, italicizing, or using all capital letters.
- Include contextual images with text.
- Left-align text for readability.

Links

- Use consistent link styles that are differentiated from other text, such as underlining links, a common web convention recognized by most users.
- Use descriptive link text.
- Include a "skip to main content" link.

Images

- Avoid using images that are purely decorative. Include empty alt tags (alt=" ") if images do not provide any actual information.
- Use text labels with icons or menu buttons.

Forms and User Inputs

- Use form validation.
- Make forms accessible with labels, instructions, and clear error messages.

Multimedia Content

- Provide captions and transcription with any audio or video content.
- Avoid flashing content and provide a play/pause button for any multimedia content.
- Don't have audio or video content automatically play when the page is loaded.

User Assistance

- Include multiple contact options, such as phone number, email, and chat.
- Provide users with rapid and direct feedback.
- Provide ways for the user to easily get help or give feedback.

EVALUATING ACCESSIBILITY

Automated evaluation tools can be helpful in locating accessibility issues and can sometimes also offer recommendations for fixing these issues. The results of an automated accessibility evaluation will generally flag your website content for both errors and warnings. Errors occur when the application detects an accessibility barrier in the website code, while warnings occur when the code may contain accessibility barriers, but a human being is needed to verify whether there is an error or not.

For this reason, successfully evaluating the accessibility of your website requires a three-pronged approach for the most accurate results. Ensuring your website meets all required accessibility guidelines requires a combination of automated testing, manual testing, and user testing.

1. Automated Testing

    Automated testing involves using one of the accessibility evaluation tools that are available online or for download. These tools generally analyze the underlying code of the website and can usually detect basic accessibility issues. However, because these tools are only looking at the code rather than the website as a whole, they can miss many issues that may cause barriers to users with disabilities. However, they usually run relatively quickly and in some cases are free, making them a great way to save time and money while locating the most egregious accessibility issues.

2. Manual Testing

    Manual testing involves having a designated person or persons evaluate the website based on a specific set of guidelines, such as WCAG. This

should be done by those involved in the web design project throughout the process to quickly identify potential issues in the design early on. An accessibility consultant can also be hired to evaluate the entire website manually once the design is complete.
3. User Testing

User testing for accessibility is similar to general usability testing, except that the participants should be people who have some type of disability or use assistive technology. Then, using the same type of prompts as in general user testing, the participants should be led through a list of tasks and provide feedback on barriers they encounter in using the website. User testing can be a time-intensive process, from recruiting participants to having someone lead them through thirty-minute tests. However, user testing is likely to be the most accurate way of testing because it uses actual website users in real-life scenarios using various assistive technology devices to perform the type of tasks that any website user would need to complete. Any accessibility barriers are likely to become apparent for these users relatively quickly.

Online Accessibility Tools

There are a number of tools available online that can be used to automate the evaluation of a website's accessibility. The following accessibility tools are free, though some offer paid options with additional or unlimited features. Also included is the W3C Web Accessibility Evaluation Tools List, which includes over one hundred additional tools.

- Accessibility Checker
  https://www.accessibilitychecker.org/
  Accessibility Checker is an online tool that audits your website against WCAG 2.1 Level AA guidelines. After entering your website's domain and running the evaluation, you receive a detailed report with explanations of accessibility errors and solutions for correcting them. The free version allows for up to two scans per day, but there are also paid plans that offer higher scan limits and downloadable reports.
- Siteimprove Accessibility Checker Extension
  https://www.siteimprove.com/integrations/browser-extensions/
  Siteimprove offers a free Accessibility Checker browser extension for checking website accessibility, available to download for Chrome, Opera, Edge, and Firefox. The analysis is performed within the browser and highlights accessibility issues with explanations as well as tips and recommendations for correcting accessibility problems.
- The A11y Machine
  https://github.com/liip/TheA11yMachine

The A11y Machine is an automated accessibility testing tool available for free download through Github. The software needs to be installed and run locally, after which it can validate web pages against WCAG 2.0 guidelines, Section 508 legislation, and W3C HTML5 recommendations.
- WAVE Web Accessibility Evaluation Tools
    https://wave.webaim.org/
    WAVE is a free online service from WebAIM (Web Accessibility in Mind) at Utah State University. It includes a suite of evaluation tools for identifying accessibility and WCAG errors, such as a browser extension (available for Chrome, Firefox, and Edge), an API and Testing Engine, and an Accessibility Impact Report.
- W3C Web Accessibility Evaluation Tools List
    https://www.w3.org/WAI/ER/tools/
    The W3C has put together this list of website accessibility evaluation tools, which include both online and downloadable software programs. The list can be filtered to find the best tool for your needs, including filters for guidelines (WCAG 2.1, Section 508), languages, and type of tool (desktop app, mobile app, online tool). The list currently includes 166 different tools, so the W3C also provides a guide for how to select the best evaluation tool for your needs (https://www.w3.org/WAI/test-evaluate/tools/selecting/).

ADDITIONAL RESOURCES

The following suggestions for further study include books that offer more in-depth information about accessibility planning and universal design, as well as links to the complete WCAG 2.2 and WAI-ARIA 1.2 guidelines, and other websites with additional information.

- "Accessible Rich Internet Applications (WAI-ARIA) 1.2." W3C Recommendation. https://www.w3.org/TR/wai-aria/.
- "Accessibility Basics." Usability.gov. https://www.usability.gov/what-and-why/accessibility.html.
- Chisholm, Wendy, and Matt May. *Universal Design for Web Applications: Web Applications That Reach Everyone*. Sebastopol, CA: O'Reilly Media, Inc., 2008.
- "Guidance on Web Accessibility and the ADA." U.S. Department of Justice Civil Rights Division. https://www.ada.gov/resources/web-guidance/.
- "Introduction to Web Accessibility." World Wide Web Consortium. https://www.w3.org/WAI/fundamentals/accessibility-intro/.

- Marrall, Rebecca M. *Developing a Library Accessibility Plan: A Practical Guide for Librarians.* Practical Guides for Librarians. Lanham: Rowman & Littlefield, 2020.
- "Web Content Accessibility Guidelines (WCAG) 2.2." W3C Recommendation. https://www.w3.org/TR/WCAG22/.
- The Centre for Excellence in Universal Design, https://universaldesign.ie/.

NOTES

1. "Disability Impacts All of Us," Centers for Disease Control and Prevention, Disability and Health Promotion, June 14, 2021, https://www.cdc.gov/ncbddd/disabilityandhealth/infographic-disability-impacts-all.html
2. "Web Accessibility Law and the ADA," Reciteme.com, March 6, 2023, https://reciteme.com/us/news/ada-web-accessibility-law/.
3. "2023 ADA Web Accessibility Standards & Requirements," Accessibility.works, June 30, 2023, https://www.accessibility.works/blog/2023-wcag-ada-website-compliance-standards-requirements/.
4. "Introduction to Web Accessibility," World Wide Web Consortium, March 31, 2022, https://www.w3.org/WAI/fundamentals/accessibility-intro/.
5. "Accessibility Basics," Usability.gov, accessed October 23, 2023, https://www.usability.gov/what-and-why/accessibility.html.
6. "Web Content Accessibility Guidelines (WCAG) 2.2," W3C Recommendation, October 5, 2023, https://www.w3.org/TR/WCAG22/.
7. Accessibility.works.
8. "Introduction to Understanding WCAG," World Wide Web Consortium, June 20, 2023, https://www.w3.org/WAI/WCAG21/Understanding/intro#understanding-the-four-principles-of-accessibility.
9. "What Is Universal Design," Centre for Excellence in Universal Design, accessed October 24, 2023, https://universaldesign.ie/what-is-universal-design/.
10. "The 7 Principles," Centre for Excellence in Universal Design, accessed October 24, 2023, https://universaldesign.ie/what-is-universal-design/the-7-principles/.

BIBLIOGRAPHY

"2023 ADA Web Accessibility Standards & Requirements." Accessibility.works. June 30, 2023. https://www.accessibility.works/blog/2023-wcag-ada-website-compliance-standards-requirements/.

"Accessibility Basics." Usability.gov. Accessed October 23, 2023. https://www.usability.gov/what-and-why/accessibility.html.

"Disability Impacts All of Us." Centers for Disease Control and Prevention, Disability and Health Promotion. June 14, 2021. https://www.cdc.gov/ncbddd/disabilityandhealth/infographic-disability-impacts-all.html.

"Introduction to Understanding WCAG." World Wide Web Consortium. June 20, 2023. https://www.w3.org/WAI/WCAG21/Understanding/intro#understanding-the-four-principles-of-accessibility.

"Introduction to Web Accessibility." World Wide Web Consortium. March 31, 2022. https://www.w3.org/WAI/fundamentals/accessibility-intro/.

"The 7 Principles." Centre for Excellence in Universal Design. Accessed October 24, 2023. https://universaldesign.ie/what-is-universal-design/the-7-principles/.

"Web Accessibility Law and the ADA." Reciteme.com. March 6, 2023. https://reciteme.com/us/news/ada-web-accessibility-law/.

"Web Content Accessibility Guidelines (WCAG) 2.2." W3C Recommendation. October 5, 2023. https://www.w3.org/TR/WCAG22/.

"What is Universal Design." Centre for Excellence in Universal Design. Accessed October 24, 2023. https://universaldesign.ie/what-is-universal-design/.

8

Website Security and Data Privacy

When creating or updating a website, it is important to make sure that certain security precautions are in place to protect it, as well as sensitive patron data, from attack. "One of the challenges facing libraries is the perception that a library's basic website and online catalog functions don't need enhanced security."[1] However, over 2,200 cyberattacks occur online each day, or roughly one every thirty-nine seconds.[2]

Keeping patron data confidential is one of librarianship's core values, and a breach of personal data can lead to patron distrust. Having your website attacked can also result in a loss of availability, website defacement, compromise of organizational data, losing control of the website, or the website being used as a platform to launch additional attacks.[3]

Website security is important whether the site is hosted on your own local servers, or by a third-party web hosting company, and whether or not your website was built using a CMS. There are many different security vulnerabilities that can make a website susceptible to attack, but some of the most common causes of attack include:

- Using weak passwords
- Incorrectly setting file permissions
- Unsecured web hosting
- Using an outdated version of WordPress or outdated WordPress plugin

The field of cybersecurity has been growing exponentially as more and more of our activities and data are focused around the internet. There are now numerous resources available online that can be used to strengthen and secure your website against attack. In addition, with users more and more concerned about the privacy of their data, libraries now more than ever need to include a patron privacy policy on their web properties. The American Library

Association has advised that libraries "should give users options as to how much information is collected from them and how it may be used" and that users "should be notified about library privacy policies when using a library website."[4]

While the field of cybersecurity is primarily focused on business environments, researchers and professional associations have also been studying security and privacy specifically in libraries and working on standardized guidelines, policies, and recommendations. Some of the current research has found that there is "little to no evidence that libraries are aware of the associated vulnerabilities, threats or risks,"[5] but other research has resulted in library-specific assessment models, such as LISSAM (Library Information Systems Security Assessment Model) based on technological and organizational measures, including security measures for workstations, servers, hardware, software, data, and networks, and the establishment of policies, procedures, and controls[6] to help guide libraries toward better systems security.

Both inside and outside of libraries, security experts tend to agree that awareness is a crucial aspect of security. In order to secure your website and protect patron data, you must first know what types of attacks to prepare for, and then how to secure your website against them.

COMMON WEBSITE SECURITY ATTACKS

Website hackers are constantly coming up with new methods to get past website security measures as security experts accordingly find new ways to prevent them. One of the most frequent ways that an attacker gains access to a website or server is through user input. This type of attack is especially common because it doesn't require the attacker to breach any network security, firewalls, or authentication. In fact, these types of attacks can be hard to detect until the damage has already been done. For example, if your website contains a web form that submits information to a database using SQL commands, an attacker could use this to submit their own SQL commands to the database. By entering an apostrophe or semicolon in the web form, which the server can interpret as a SQL line-break command, the attacker can gain full access to the database. From there they can do things like delete data or drop entire tables of data altogether.

There are ways to prevent attacks that make use of user input, such as sanitizing user input before it is submitted to the database. Sanitizing input involves testing the input for data type, expected values, or unnecessary characters, and not allowing the submission of data if it doesn't meet these criteria. Many web languages, such as PHP, which is often used in conjunction with SQL, have specific functions that can be used to protect against these injection attacks. For example, PHP includes a function to convert special characters to HTML entities, and another to remove single and double quote characters from a string.

When rejecting user input from a web form, it is better to provide specific error messages through the application, rather than relying on system-generated error messages. System-generated messages can contain server information that may help an attacker exploit the system. PHP provides detailed system-generated error messages to help developers debug applications during development, but these messages should be disabled on the production site so that attackers aren't able to use this information to exploit the system.

While user input is often an easy way for criminals to gain access to a server, there are many different types of cyberattacks in use today. Some of the most common types of attacks are listed here.

SQL/Code Injection

In a SQL or code injection attack, the attacker inserts SQL commands or a malicious script into a form input on the website. This can cause the attacker to be given unauthorized access to the database or the ability to execute system commands, which can give them full control of the database or the entire application.

Cross-Site Scripting (XSS)

Cross-site scripting is a client-side code injection attack in which the attacker attaches code to a legitimate website that executes when the user visits the site. A cross-site scripting attack can be used to extract data, install malware, or redirect the user to a different website altogether.

Cross-Site Request Forgery (CSRF)

A cross-site request forgery attempts to trick a user into accidently using their credentials to perform some action for the attacker, such as transferring bank funds or changing their password. If a user is already authenticated in a system and then clicks on a link or email sent by an attacker, the attacker can then use that to send a request to the system, which gets executed because of the user's prior authentication. If the user has an admin account, the attacker will be able to gain access to the entire application and perform any actions the user is authorized to perform.

Session Hijacking

Session hijacking is similar to cross-site request forgery, but it involves the attacker stealing a user's session cookie and using it to gain access to their session ID. With the session ID, the attacker is able to perform actions on the website as though they are the original user, such as transferring money, making purchases, or accessing the user's personal data.

Broken Authentication/ Password-Based Attacks

A broken authentication or password-based attack is any login access that is gained illegitimately, such as through compromised credentials. This can be done through various methods such as a brute force attack (systematically guessing various passwords), credential stuffing (using known credentials from another site), or dictionary attacks (using a dictionary of common passwords). A compromised password can be particularly dangerous for organizations that use single sign-on authentication, as this can result in the attacker being authenticated for multiple applications after stealing a single password.

Drive-By Download

A drive-by download is when a user visits a page and malware is automatically downloaded onto their computer. This type of automatic download can also occur when a user is downloading something else, when they open an infected email, or when they click on a pop-up.

Fuzzing

In a fuzzing attack, the attacker inputs a large amount of random data into an application, causing it to crash, then uses a special software to identify weak spots in the application's security. They can then use these uncovered weaknesses to exploit and gain access to the system. Fuzzing is also used by security testers to find and remediate vulnerabilities before an attacker does.

Distributed Denial-of-Service

A denial-of-service attack is when the attacker bombards a server with so many requests that the server becomes unavailable for legitimate visitors. In a distributed denial-of-service attack, a network of distributed sources is used to send the requests. Bots or networks of bots distributed across multiple infected computers, known as botnets, are often used to create and send the large number of requests.

Man-in-the-Middle

A man-in-the-middle attack is when an attacker is able to eavesdrop on communication between a user and a server. The attacker can then steal the information being transferred, such as credentials, account numbers, or passwords. As the man-in-the-middle of the conversation, the attacker can also impersonate one of the parties or alter the communication between them without either party knowing.

Insecure Direct Object References (IDOR)

Insecure direct object reference occurs when an application inadvertently provides direct access to objects such as a database or files. This sometimes happens based on direct user input, such as changing a portion of a web address to view a different file. By doing this, the user is able to bypass any authentication and gain access to data that is not meant to be available to them.

Directory Traversal

A type of IDOR attack, directory traversal is when an attacker is able to access unauthorized files or directories by attacking the web root folder and moving up within the file hierarchy. This can allow an attacker access to configuration files, user credentials, or even a functional shell on the target server.

Exploiting Known Vulnerabilities

Some code or applications are known to have specific security flaws that can be used in an attack. Often new versions of web languages or software patches will fix these known flaws, but if you don't keep your system updated, an attacker can exploit them to gain access to the system.

Preventing Common Security Issues

With the number of cyberattacks growing every year, it's important to take precautions to prevent the most common types of attacks. A good web hosting company will already take care of some security precautions, such as providing an SSL certificate, but if you're using your own server or writing your own code, it is vital to use known security methods to ensure your website or system is secure.

Table 8.1 provides commonly used methods to prevent some of the most common types of cyberattacks.

BEST PRACTICES FOR WEBSITE SECURITY

When it comes to managing website security, there are a number of commonly accepted best practices. The National Institute of Standards and Technology (NIST) has issued a "Guide to General Server Security," which goes through all the server configurations and settings needed to secure any type of server. There are also freely available guidelines online that detail how to specifically secure a Linux or Windows server or operating system. Implementing security

Table 8.1 Common security threats and how to prevent them.

Security Threat	How to Prevent
Injection flaws/ cross-site scripting	• Limit functions that are permissible through SQL commands. • Filter/sanitize user input—validate form input data to make sure it is what you're expecting, strip/escape content so that HTML or script tags are not passed through, don't allow special characters or symbols.
Broken authentication/ password	• Use a framework for authenticating users rather than trying to build your own. • Use secure passwords. • Use multi-factor authentication. • Store passwords as hash values such as SHA2, not in plain text.
Drive-by downloads	• Keep applications, browsers, and operating systems up-to-date. • Limit the use of plugins. • Disable or remove applications that are not being used from the server.
Insecure direct object references	• Always authenticate users before providing access to any data. • Avoid direct object references. • Validate all user input.
Directory traversal	• Don't pass user input to filesystem APIs. • Limit directory browsing. • Sanitize all user input.
Cross-site request forgery	• Use secret tokens that can verify the authorized user is submitting the form and not an unauthorized third party.
Distributed denial-of-service	• Use content delivery networks or load balancers to mitigate traffic. • Use a web application firewall.
Man-in-the-middle	• Install an SSL certificate so that all data is encrypted.
Fuzzing	• Install all software security patches and updates.
Exploitation of known vulnerabilities	• Don't copy and paste code from third-party sites without checking it first. • Keep software up-to-date.

measures on a server is known as server hardening. Some frequently recommended best practices for server security are listed below.

- Research and select a secure web-hosting provider.
- Regularly back up website content.
- Sanitize and validate all user input when using web forms.
- Change the default admin username and password.
- Use the "Principle of Least Privilege" to give users only the permissions they need to do their job and none that they don't need.
- Create strong passwords and keep them protected.
- Limit the number of login attempts allowed in a session.
- Implement two-factor/multi-factor authentication systems.
- Remove unused software from the server.
- Minimize the number of open ports on the server and shut down any unused interfaces.
- Install an SSL certificate and use HTTPS on all web properties.
- Use a web application firewall.
- Use a security plugin if your site is built in WordPress.
- Update software, install security patches, replace unsupported systems and applications, and enable automatic software updates whenever possible.
- Regularly scan for malware and viruses and keep anti-malware and anti-virus software up-to-date.
- Keep and monitor website logs for suspicious activity.
- Only collect data that you actually plan to use, and don't store personal information in perpetuity.

Creating Strong Passwords

When it comes to protecting online applications or data, the first line of defense is a strong password. Any default passwords should be changed immediately so attackers aren't able to use a known admin password to gain access. In addition, use best practices when creating passwords to make it as difficult as possible for an attacker to guess. The most frequently used passwords are "123456," followed by "password" and "abc123." Using these types of passwords is almost a guarantee that your account will be hacked. Instead, a strong password uses a mix of letters, numbers, and symbols, and doesn't spell out any actual words. For example, "m#P52s@ap$V" is hard to remember, but also hard to guess.

Using a brute-force attack algorithm, a hacker can crack an eight-character password consisting of only lowercase letters in 0.19 milliseconds. Adding a mix of letters and numbers increases that time to forty-one years, while adding special characters increases it to sixty-three thousand years. And while complexity is extremely important, ultimately the length of the password makes the most difference in its security. An eight-character password consisting of a mix of numbers, upper- and lower-case letters, and special characters would take a hacker five minutes to crack but using the same complexity in a sixteen-character password increases that time to five billion years.[7]

Some best practices for creating strong passwords include:

- Don't use personal information in your password (like your birthday or name).
- Don't use common passwords or words found in the dictionary.
- Use a different password for every account.
- Make your password at least sixteen characters long, or as long as is permitted by the system.
- Use mnemonic devices to create complex passwords and a way to remember them.
- Use complexity to create a unique password, with mixed cases, numbers, and special characters.
- Use two-factor authentication.
- Change your password if you find it's been compromised.

In the past, security experts recommended changing your password every three months; however, more recently they have abandoned this recommendation, since frequently changing passwords leads to users needing to write their password down, negating any additional security. Instead, they now recommend creating a password that is as unique and complex as possible so that potential attackers aren't able to guess or deduce what it is and using a password manager to track these unique passwords across sites.

Password managers are software that can be used to manage all your passwords within a single application. When using a password manager, you only have to remember one password. But it needs to be a really good password; otherwise, every account with a password saved by the software will be at risk. Some frequently used password managers include:

- LastPass: https://lastpass.com/
- KeePass: https://keepass.info/
- Keeper: https://keepersecurity.com
- Password Safe: https://pwsafe.org/
- Dashlane: https://dashlane.com/
- 1Password: https://1password.com/
- Bitwarden: https://bitwarden.com/

Attackers will use a variety of methods to try to guess, steal, or crack your password. Having a complex password and an awareness of password security can go a long way toward preventing this. Some of the most common methods attackers to use to try to gain access to your password include:

- Phishing: When an attacker poses as a trustworthy party to trick you into revealing your password, such as through a fraudulent email.
- Man-in-the-Middle attacks: When an attacker intercepts an unencrypted password being exchanged between systems.
- Brute Force attack: When an attacker uses software to try millions of potential password/username combinations in a short amount of time.
- Dictionary attack: When an attacker uses a "dictionary" of basic and common passwords in a brute-force attack.
- Credential Stuffing: When an attacker uses formerly leaked passwords to try to access other accounts in the hope that the user never updated them.

It can be a good idea to occasionally check on the integrity of your accounts to see if your account or password has been compromised. There are sites available online that can inform you whether your account has been involved in a known security breach. Some of these sites include:

- Have I Been Pwned: https://haveibeenpwned.com/
- Firefox Monitor: https://monitor.mozilla.org/
- Google Password Checkup: https://passwords.google.com/checkup/start?ep=1&pr=sa (sign in and select Go to Password Checkup)

SECURITY TESTING

Methods for testing your website's security include both manual and automated testing options. Manual testing requires an expertise in cybersecurity and involves manually trying to exploit vulnerabilities on the website or auditing the site against common security benchmarks. While manual testing is labor-intensive and requires hiring an expert, it can uncover complex vulnerabilities that automated testing may miss.

The simplest type of automated testing is vulnerability scanning, which involves using software to scan a website for common vulnerabilities and security flaws. Since attackers can also use vulnerability scanning software, it is important to find and remediate these vulnerabilities as soon as they are discovered.

Another automated type of testing is fuzz testing (fuzzing), which uses software to inject invalid or unexpected input into the system and then monitors the system for crashes or information leaks. Since user input is the source of many malicious attacks, fuzz testing can help to find these types of vulnerabilities before an attacker does. While automated testing makes the process much quicker and easier, these tools can sometimes generate false positives or miss more complex vulnerabilities.

In addition to automated scanning for vulnerabilities, some organizations use penetration testing (or pen testing) to test for vulnerabilities in their network or system. During penetration testing, a cybersecurity expert or experts try to hack into the system by looking for vulnerabilities they can exploit. Penetration testing is basically a simulated attack using the same tools an attacker would use, by experts with the same type of knowledge. Often penetration testing is performed by a separate company that specializes in cybersecurity.

The following resources include standard checklists that can be used to manually check that your server or website is secured, as well as a list of online automated tools that can be used to automatically scan for vulnerabilities.

Benchmarks and Checklists

- SANS Institute Securing Web Application Technologies Checklist (SWAT)
    https://www.sans.org/cloud-security/securing-web-application-technologies/
    The SANS (SysAdmin, Audit, Network, and Security) Institute's checklist of best practices for web application security.
- OWASP Web Application Security Testing Checklist
    https://github.com/0xRadi/OWASP-Web-Checklist
    OWASP's (The Open Worldwide Application Security Project) checklist for manually testing web application servers.
- Center for Internet Security Benchmarks Lists
    https://www.cisecurity.org/cis-benchmarks
    Server configuration recommendations for multiple products, such as cloud providers, server software, and operating systems, including a variety of Windows and Linux systems.
- Microsoft Security Compliance Toolkit and Baselines
    https://www.microsoft.com/en-us/download/details.aspx?id=55319
    A set of tools provided by Microsoft with recommended security configuration baselines for Windows servers.

Online Automated Tools

- Qualys SSL Server Test
    https://www.ssllabs.com/ssltest/
    Qualys started as a SaaS security company and created the SSL Labs, which offers a collection of documents and tools related to SSL security. The SSL Server Test is a free online service that tests the SSL configuration of any web server on the internet and provides an A–F rating on the strength of its security.
- Qualys Web Application Scanning
    https://www.qualys.com/apps/web-app-scanning/

Another service offered by Qualys is their Web Application Scanning product, which can scan any website to find vulnerabilities, misconfigurations, PII exposures, and malware. They offer a free trial, but to receive a quote for the service you must contact the company.

- Pentest Tools Website Vulnerability Scanner

    https://pentest-tools.com/website-vulnerability-scanning/website-scanner

    Pentest Tools is a security company that offers the Pentest-Tools.com website as a penetration testing and vulnerability assessment platform. Their Website Vulnerability Scanner can detect XSS, SQL injection, command injection, and other critical security flaws. There is a free option as well as several paid tiers.

- OWASP Vulnerability Scanning Tools

    https://owasp.org/www-community/Vulnerability_Scanning_Tools

    OWASP has put together this list of web application vulnerability scanners currently available on the market. The list includes the product name and company, on what platforms each can be used, and whether they are commercial or freely available. Some include notes about free trial periods or free options of commercial versions of the software.

DATA PRIVACY

The right to privacy has long been a standard of the American Library Association, whose Code of Ethics states, "we protect each library user's right to privacy and confidentiality."[8] The ALA has published several resources to assist libraries in safeguarding users' privacy, such as their "Privacy Guidelines and Checklists" and the "Privacy Tool Kit."

The general information security sector also has many resources that can be applied toward data privacy and security in libraries. A guiding model for information security from the National Institute of Standards and Technology that is used by many organizations is the CIA triad.[9] The CIA triad consists of the components Confidentiality, Integrity, and Availability, and it forms the basis for information security.

Libraries ensure their users' data is protected in a number of ways. In *Library Privacy Policies*, Jason Vaughan advises libraries to implement organizational measures to limit access and protect data, as well as "technical security measures like encrypting transmitted and stored data, limiting access by using passwords, and storing data on secure servers."[10] Vaughan notes that most libraries will also need to follow policies approved by their consortium or system, board of trustees, or university.

The ALA's "Privacy Tool Kit" notes special privacy considerations that should be taken into account depending on library type. Some of these considerations include:

- Academic Libraries
  - Intellectual freedom
  - FERPA (Family Educational Rights and Privacy Act)
- School Libraries
  - FERPA (Family Educational Rights and Privacy Act)
  - COPPA (Children's Online Privacy Protection Act)
- Public Libraries
  - State-enacted laws on the rights of minors
  - COPPA (Children's Online Privacy Protection Act)
- Special Libraries
  - ASCLA Statement of Privacy Rights

Conducting a Privacy Audit

While libraries will want to ensure that they have a library privacy policy available on their website, it can help to first perform a privacy audit to ensure that privacy and confidentiality practices are in line with the library's goals. A privacy audit examines "how the library collects, stores, shares, uses, and

Table 8.2   Components of the CIA triad.

Component	Definition	Implementation
Confidentiality	Sensitive data is protected from unauthorized access.	• Have and follow data-handling security policies. • Use encryption and multi-factor authentication. • Make sure file permissions are up-to-date.
Integrity	Data is accurate and trustworthy and has not been illegitimately changed.	• Ensure employee security awareness to minimize human error. • Regularly back up important data. • Use version control and access control.
Availability	Data is readily accessible to authorized users.	• Keep systems and applications updated. • Monitor activity on servers or networks for potential security breaches.

destroys information about library users and employees."[11] The ALA recommends examining a variety of record types, files, and logs during a privacy audit, including:

- Patron records, circulation and interlibrary loan transactions, and billing records
- Searches and reference questions
- Usage statistics of electronic resources/databases and proxy server statistics
- Personalized profiles, services, bookmarks, and tags

When auditing the library's data and data privacy, the following questions should be considered:

- Is the collection of personally identifiable information (PII) limited to only what is necessary?
- Is there a time limit for record retention, and how is data deleted or destroyed?
- Are records and data currently protected from unauthorized access and how?
- Are patrons notified when their PII is being collected and given the choice to opt out?
- Are minors given the same (or the legally allowable) degree of privacy protection as adults?
- Have employees been educated about data privacy issues and their responsibility for protecting PII?

WRITING A DATA PRIVACY POLICY

There are several important steps to writing a data privacy policy, as well as some generally accepted best practices. A privacy policy should be written in clear and easy-to-understand language and minimize the use of technical jargon or legal terminology. The major sections that any privacy policy will need to include are:

- What information is collected (and whether any of it is sensitive or PII)
- Why the data is collected
- How the data is collected
- How the data will be used
- How you will inform users about changes to the policy
- How users can contact the library with questions or concerns
- How you will protect this data

The ALA's "Privacy Tool Kit" includes other sections that they recommend specifically for library privacy policies. These sections include:

- Notice and Openness: Notify users of their right to privacy and confidentiality.
- Choice and Consent: Give users the choice about how and whether their information can be used.
- Access by Users: Mention users' right to access their own information.
- Emerging Technologies with Privacy Concerns: Address technologies that may cause privacy issues and how (such as through the apps, cameras, cell phones, cloud computing, ebooks and ejournals, elearning, OPACs, RFID/NFC, and social media).
- Data Integrity and Security: Describe how data is protected.
- Enforcement and Redress: Discuss how the privacy policy is enforced and what redress is available to users.
- Government Requests for Library Records: Describe how the library will respond to government requests for private information and what legal conditions would require the library to release data.

Writing a privacy policy may seem overwhelming; however, there is no need to start from scratch. There are many, many library privacy policies that have been written and made freely available on the open web. A quick search will bring up numerous examples. In addition, the Library Freedom Project has created a privacy policy template that can be used by any library for creating their own policy. That template can be accessed at https://bit.ly/LFIprivacytemp.

ADDITIONAL RESOURCES

- Cybersecurity and Infrastructure Security Agency. "Cybersecurity Alerts & Advisories." https://www.cisa.gov/uscert/ncas/alerts.
- The Open Worldwide Application Security Project (OWASP). https://owasp.org/.
- American Library Association. "Privacy Tool Kit." January 2014. https://alair.ala.org/handle/11213/16714.
- American Library Association. "Guidelines & Checklists." January 2017. https://www.ala.org/advocacy/privacy/guidelineschecklists.
- Berman, Erin and Bonnie Tijerina. "Privacy Field Guides for Libraries." https://libraryprivacyguides.org/privacy-policies/.
- Vaughan, Jason. "Library Privacy Policies." *Library Technology Reports* 56, no. 6 (2020): 1–56. https://doi.org/10.5860/ltr.56n6.
- Library Freedom Project. https://libraryfreedom.org/.

NOTES

1. Richard Thomchick and Tonia San Nicholas-Rocca, "Application Level Security in a Public Library: A Case Study," *Information Technology and Libraries 37*, no. 4 (2018): 110, https://doi.org/10.6017/ital.v37i4.10405.
2. Jacob Fox, "Top Cybersecurity Statistics for 2024," Cobalt, December 8, 2023, https://www.cobalt.io/blog/cybersecurity-statistics-2024.
3. Cybersecurity & Infrastructure Security Agency, "Website Security," February 1, 2021, https://www.cisa.gov/news-events/news/website-security.
4. American Library Association, "Library Privacy Guidelines for Library Websites, OPACs, and Discovery Services," January 26, 2020, https://www.ala.org/advocacy/privacy/guidelines/OPAC.
5. Thomchick & Nicholas-Rocca, 110.
6. Roesnita Ismail and Awang Ngah Zainab, "Assessing the Status of Library Information Systems Security," *Journal of Librarianship and Information Science 45*, no. 3 (2013): 232–47, https://doi.org/10.1177/0961000613477676.
7. Lance Whitney, "How an 8-Character Password Could Be Cracked in Just a Few Minutes," TechRepublic, January 18, 2024, https://www.techrepublic.com/article/how-an-8-character-password-could-be-cracked-in-less-than-an-hour/.
8. American Library Association, "Code of Ethics," June 29, 2021, https://www.ala.org/tools/ethics.
9. National Institute of Standards and Technology, "Data Integrity: Detecting and Responding to Ransomware and Other Destructive Events," December 2020, https://www.nccoe.nist.gov/publication/1800-26/VolA/index.html.
10. Jason Vaughan, "Library Privacy Policies," *Library Technology Reports 56*, no. 6 (2020): 36, https://doi.org/10.5860/ltr.56n6.
11. American Library Association, "Privacy Tool Kit," January 2014: 8, https://alair.ala.org/handle/11213/16714.

BIBLIOGRAPHY

American Library Association. "Code of Ethics." June 29, 2021. https://www.ala.org/tools/ethics.

American Library Association. "Library Privacy Guidelines for Library Websites, OPACs, and Discovery Services." January 26, 2020. https://www.ala.org/advocacy/privacy/guidelines/OPAC.

American Library Association. "Privacy Tool Kit." January 2014. https://alair.ala.org/handle/11213/16714.

Cybersecurity & Infrastructure Security Agency. "Website Security." February 1, 2021. https://www.cisa.gov/news-events/news/website-security.

Fox, Jacob. "Top Cybersecurity Statistics for 2024." Cobalt. December 8, 2023. https://www.cobalt.io/blog/cybersecurity-statistics-2024.

Ismail, Roesnita and Awang Ngah Zainab. "Assessing the Status of Library Information Systems Security." *Journal of Librarianship and Information Science 45*, no. 3 (2013): 232–47. https://doi.org/10.1177/0961000613477676.

National Institute of Standards and Technology. "Data Integrity: Detecting and Responding to Ransomware and Other Destructive Events." December 2020. https://www.nccoe.nist.gov/publication/1800-26/VolA/index.html.

Thomchick, Richard, and Tonia San Nicholas-Rocca. "Application Level Security in a Public Library: A Case Study." *Information Technology and Libraries* 37, no. 4 (2018): 107–18. https://doi.org/10.6017/ital.v37i4.10405.

Vaughan, Jason. "Library Privacy Policies." *Library Technology Reports* 56, no. 6 (2020). https://doi.org/10.5860/ltr.56n6.

Whitney, Lance. "How an 8-Character Password Could Be Cracked in Just a Few Minutes." TechRepublic. January 18, 2024. https://www.techrepublic.com/article/how-an-8-character-password-could-be-cracked-in-less-than-an-hour/.

9

Assessment and Analytics

After designing, testing, and launching a new website, you will want to know how well the new website is performing and whether or not it's meeting the needs of your users. However, assessment should not be a onetime event that happens after the launch of the website and then never again. Instead, there should be a continuous process of assessment that leads to ongoing, incremental improvements of the site. Continuous assessment with frequent small changes can prevent the website from getting too out-of-date and can also prevent or postpone the need for another full-scale redesign project for some time.

There are many different aspects of a website that can be assessed, and each is important in its own way. While website analytics tools often track metrics that can be used to assess site performance or search engine optimization, it is vital to assess other things, such as a website's usability, accessibility, and security as well.

Table 9.1 lists each type of assessment with some of the most used assessment methods for that type.

While previous chapters have focused on usability, accessibility, and security, including how to assess each of these more in depth, the rest of this chapter will focus on assessing site performance using analytics data.

WEBSITE ANALYTICS

There are many benefits to assessing your website, including using website analytics data to measure the use of your site in quantitative terms. *Website analytics* "is the measurement, collection, analysis, and reporting of internet data for the purposes of understanding and optimizing web usage."[1] Analytics data can help you learn more about your website visitors, improve the user

Table 9.1   Types and methods of website assessment.

Assessment Type	Methods
Usability	• User testing • Card sorting • Interviews • First-click testing • Usability testing tools (Optimal Workshop, Optimizely, UserZoom)
Accessibility	• WCAG guidelines • ADA and Section 508 guidelines • Accessibility testing tools (WAVE, Accessibility Checker, Siteimprove)
Security	• Website security benchmarks (SANS, OWASP, CIS, Microsoft) • Penetration testing • Security testing tools (Qualys SSL Labs, Pentest Tools, OWASP tools)
Search engine optimization	• A/B testing • Multivariate testing • Testing page speed, URL optimization, image optimization, mobile friendliness, and meta tags • SEO testing tools (Ahrefs, SEMrush, SEOptimer, Google PageSpeed Insights)
Site performance	• Surveys • Focus groups • Web logs/proxy server logs • Reference stats • Heatmapping • Analytics data • Website analytics tools (Google Analytics, Matomo, Open Web Analytics)

experience, increase search engine optimization, and determine whether users are ultimately getting what they need from the site.

When assessing site performance, quantitative data, such as website analytics, can provide you with a variety of metrics to use to benchmark and assess your website. However, analytics data can only tell part of the story. To gain a full understanding of how well your site is performing, it is important to collect and assess qualitative data as well. While quantitative data can tell you how many users visit your site, what pages they go to, and what browser and device they are using, it can't tell you anything about why users do what they do or whether or not they like the site.

Qualitative data can give you a way to look at analytics data within its context and adds insights that purely quantitative data can't provide. Some online analytics tools, such as Hotjar, can provide qualitative data alongside other quantitative metrics. You can also use qualitative data methods such as surveys, interviews, and focus groups to gather more information about how users think and feel about your website.

When first collecting analytics data, it is recommended that you track data over the course of a full year "in order to establish a statistical baseline."[2] Once a baseline is established, it will provide more context to the data you collect as you will be able to track changes and trends year over year.

COMMON METRICS

There are a number of different quantitative metrics that can be used to assess a website's performance. Most of the more popular website analytics tools will track and aggregate data from the most common metrics, as these tend to be the most useful for determining performance information about your site, such as which pages are the most viewed, which pages are viewed for the longest duration of time, and how many of your site visitors are new users versus returning users. Each metric can provide information about your site that can be used to analyze how well the website is performing and if and where any changes may need to be made.

Some common analytics metrics include:

- Pageviews: Sometimes called impressions, *pageviews* are the total number of times a page was viewed within a given time frame. The number of pageviews can sometimes be inflated because a view is counted every time the page is loaded in the browser, including when the user refreshes the page, or when they navigate to a different page and then return to the original.
- Unique pageviews: *Unique pageviews* may provide more accurate insight into the popularity of each website page because this metric aggregates pageviews from each user over a single session. This means that if a user reloads the page or visits the page twice during one session, it would be counted as only one unique pageview.
- Sessions: A *session* tracks all user interactions with the website during a given time frame, such as within a thirty-minute period. For some analytics platforms, a session begins when a user arrives on your site and ends when the user has been inactive for thirty minutes, or at the end of that day (midnight). If a user is inactive for more than thirty minutes and then

Assessment and Analytics

returns and starts interacting with the site again, that would be considered a new session.
- Average time on page: *Average time on page* is a calculation of the average amount of time a user spends on a page in seconds or minutes. In theory, the more engaging or relevant the content is, the longer a user will tend to spend on the page. Low average times may indicate that the site's visitors are not reading much of the content. However, this metric may not ultimately mean that much because a long average time could also mean the user walked away from their computer and left the browser open.
- Average session duration: *Average session duration* refers to the average amount of time that a user spends on the website during an entire session. Rather than the time they spend on a single page, this metric calculates the average amount of time they spend interacting with your entire website.
- Pages per session: *Pages per session* calculates the average number of pages on the website that a user visits per session. This can give you an idea of whether visitors are only viewing a small number of pages, which could mean they are looking for specific information and don't need to visit the rest of the site, or whether they are viewing multiple pages of the site during a session.
- New visitors: Also known as *unique visitors*, *new visitors* is the number of users visiting your site for the first time. This is usually tracked by placing a cookie in the user's browser, which tells the website that a user has been to the site before. These numbers can be inaccurate, though, if the user deletes cookies from their browser, or if they use different browsers or different devices to access the site.
- Returning visitors: *Returning visitors* is the number of visitors to your site who have been there before. Looking at the ratio of new-to-returning visitors can you give an idea of how many regular users you have and how many new users are coming to your site on a regular basis.
- Referring sites: Also known as traffic sources or referring URLs, *referring sites* are the sites that link users to your website. This can let you know where the majority of your visitors are coming from, whether that is a search engine, another website, or from directly typing in the site URL. Some analytics tools will also track these sites by category, such as organic search (traffic from a search engine like Google), paid search (traffic from an ad on a search engine results page), referrals (a link on another website), email marketing, social media, and direct traffic. Referrals in the direct traffic category may come from users who have bookmarked the site or typed the URL directly into the browser.
- Bounce rate: *Bounce rate* refers to the percentage of visitors who leave the website after viewing only a single page. In general terms, a bounce rate under 40 percent is considered good, while a bounce rate over 70 percent is considered high. While a high bounce rate can indicate a problem with

the site or that users aren't finding what they want when they arrive to the site, it can also indicate that users have followed a link out of the website to another domain. For libraries, this can be a good thing, if users are linking out to databases or other resources the library provides. This can indicate that users are finding the resources they need.
- Exit pages: *Exit pages* are the pages on your website that users are on before leaving the site. A page with a high number of exits could mean that most users are finding a link to an outside domain they are looking for, such as linking the user to the catalog, a database, an interlibrary loan system, or research guides hosted on another platform.
- Conversions: A *conversion* is when a site visitor takes some specific action you want to track, such as purchasing a product, signing up for a newsletter, or filling out a form. Not all websites or all website pages will have conversions as a goal, but tracking them can give you a good idea about whether the website is meeting your goals.
- Location/country: Many website analytics tools will track various demographic information about your site visitors, including their *location*, by tracking the user's IP address. Tools like Google Analytics will let you drill further into the data to see how many visitors your site gets by country, by state, or even by city. A public library website may get the majority of their visitors from the local area, while a library at a university with global or online programs may have visitors from across the world. If you find that you're receiving a high amount of traffic from an unexpected location, it could be a sign that hackers are trying to gain access to the site.
- Browser: Many website analytics tools track which web *browser* the visitor is using to access the site, such as Chrome, Firefox, Edge, Safari, Opera, or others. This data can be useful when designing your website to ensure there is cross-browser compatibility, especially for the most frequently used browsers.
- Device: Another useful metric is that of which *devices* website visitors are using to access the site. While the desktop was once the most-used device for website browsing, many websites now find that more or most users are accessing the site with some type of mobile device, such as a tablet or smartphone. This information can also be important during the design process, as you will want to ensure that the site performs well on the most frequently used device types and screen sizes.
- On/off campus: Academic libraries may want to know how many of their website visitors are students or employees who are on campus and how many are accessing the site from other locations. This can be tracked by IP address, where all of the users accessing the site from on campus will be within the same IP range. Software like EZproxy, which authenticates users for remote access to resources, can also track whether users accessing resources from behind the EZproxy login are on or off campus.

DATA-DRIVEN DECISION-MAKING

Once you've established benchmarks and collected the data, you'll need to decide what to do with that data. There is no reason to gather data if you're not going to use it, but if you do, it can be instrumental in providing the basis to perform data-driven improvements to the website. How can metrics such as pageviews, sessions, and bounce rate be used to improve the website? These are a few examples of how libraries have used analytics data to inform decisions about designing and updating their library website:

- "Data such as the hit rate, time to serve documents, and peak hits can be used to measure server load and to justify server upgrades."[3]
- Search logs can be used to determine what website visitors are trying to find[4] or to make changes to the website's keyword search.[5]
- Prominent links on the homepage that are rarely clicked on can be removed to provide space for more frequently used resources.[6]
- Visitors' connection speeds when using the site can inform how much graphical content can be added to the page without slowing down page speed.[7]
- Website subpages that are frequently landing pages can be made easier to access from other pages of the site. Pages with high numbers of visits that are not at top levels of the navigation can be moved up in the site hierarchy.[8]
- Important pages that get little use can be given greater prominence on the site.[9]

When making decisions using quantitative metrics, it's important to analyze this data in context and consider possible influences on the data that could change its meaning. For example, consider bounce rates in context with where users are going when they leave the page. Are users abandoning the page because they aren't able to find what they need? Or are they finding that link to a database or catalog they were looking for and leaving the site that way?

For many websites, a low average time spent on the site might be a signal that users aren't engaging with the site contents. However, libraries typically want users to find what they need as quickly as possible, which could easily translate to spending less time on the site. A high number of site visits could be more users suddenly visiting the site, but it could also be attributable to web crawlers, or the site being the default homepage of browsers used in a computer lab.

Because analytics do not provide answers to why users do something or how they feel about it, "web analytics are most useful when combined with other methods to confirm findings and develop interpretations."[10] This combination of data can help you interpret these metrics in a way that makes sense for your library and its users.

ANALYTICS AND USER PRIVACY

When it comes to tracking website analytics, libraries face something of a catch-22 situation. Collecting more data means having more information on hand that can be used to inform decision-making and ultimately improve the site. However, "the very act of using a third-party service to collect data on patron behavior has the potential to conflict with an ideal that has been promoted in institutional publications like the American Library Association (ALA) Code of Ethics: protecting user privacy."[11] This is something libraries must grapple with as they decide whether or not to implement analytics tracking on their library website, especially in the current climate in which internet users are more aware and concerned with their privacy than they were in the past, some even going so far as "to not use products or services out of concerns for their privacy and the personal information companies collect."[12]

To track website data while still observing the ALA Code of Ethics, scholars in the library field recommend using aggregated data rather than individual user data,[13] maintaining control of the data by using analytics tools like Matomo that don't require sharing data with a third party,[14] or making use of the privacy options included in some analytics tools, such as IP anonymization, data deletion, and Do Not Track features for users.[15]

However, "the most tangible action a librarian can take to this end seems to come in the form of crafting a website privacy policy that lets users know that certain data points about them are being collected."[16] In fact, Google includes the following as part of its Google Analytics Terms of Service:

> You must post a Privacy Policy and that Privacy Policy must provide notice of your use of cookies, identifiers for mobile devices (e.g., Android Advertising Identifier or Advertising Identifier for iOS) or similar technology used to collect data. You must disclose the use of Google Analytics, and how it collects and processes data.[17]

Google also recommends that users of Google Analytics provide their website visitors with "clear and comprehensive" information about Google's use of cookies and to have users provide consent to such data collection. This is required by Google in locations where obtaining such consent is also required by law, such as EU countries that must maintain GDPR compliance.

The use of cookies has historically been the way that web analytics tools have been able to track website usage. A cookie is simply a string of text that a website uses to identify you. When you first visit a website, if a cookie has not yet been set, one will be generated and stored in your browser. When you revisit that site, the site will recognize the cookie and remember that you have been there before. Cookies generally have an expiration, which will limit the amount of time that the browser can hold on to the cookie, as well as a scope, which limits where the cookie's value is accessible. The cookies that are placed on your browser from a website that you visit are first-party cookies; however, third-party cookies can also be placed on the browser from external resources that get loaded into the browser through that website, such as fonts, scripts, or images. First- and third-party cookies work together to track your identity between different sites, which is why if you look up a product on one domain, you may later see advertisements for that product on another website.

Recently, browser developers have been working on ways to prevent tracking of their users through cookies and better protect user privacy, all of which can have an impact on the collection of website analytics. Safari, Firefox, Edge, iOS, and Chrome have all implemented some sort of live tracking prevention that can make the collection of data more difficult. In addition to technical challenges, legal challenges to user tracking have also arisen in many jurisdictions. Some of the initiatives and regulations regarding online user privacy that have been enacted recently include:

- General Data Protection Regulation (GDPR): A 2018 data privacy regulation from Europe that protects how personal information is processed for those in the EU/EEA. The GDPR requires businesses to post a clear and transparent privacy policy that explains their data collection processes. They must also take measures to securely store the data from breaches or leaks.
- California Consumer Privacy Act (CCPA): A strict privacy law enacted in 2020 that gives California residents the ability to control how businesses process their personal information, including the right to access, delete, or opt out of sharing their data.
- Enhanced Tracking Protection (ETP): An initiative rolled out by Firefox in 2020 to protect Firefox users from redirect tracking. ETP clears cookies and site data every twenty-four hours.
- App Tracking Transparency (ATT): A user privacy framework implemented by Apple in 2021 that requires users to opt-in to share their device ID with an app developer or marketer.
- ePrivacy Regulation (ePR): An EU law that extends the GDPR by requiring all electronic communications services (including social media, email, and instant messaging) to provide users with clear information about how cookies will be used and obtain explicit consent from users before using cookies to collect data for targeted advertising. As of early 2024, the ePR has not yet passed, and it will have a twenty-four-month transition period once finalized.

Even with these hurdles, it is still possible to collect and use analytics data in an ethical way. There are a number of ways to work with analytical data that can maintain patron privacy while also allowing you to collect data for analytical purposes. Some best practices for working with website analytics data include:

1. Follow the principle of data minimization: Only collect the data that you need and nothing more. Avoid collecting any personal data that is not necessary for your purposes (name, email, address, etc.).
2. Get users' consent: Consent should be obtained by having users opt-in to the collection of their data after you have informed them of what information you will collect, how you will use it, who it will be shared with, and how long it will be retained. Users should also have the option to withdraw consent at any time.
3. Use cookies responsibly: Follow the legal guidelines for the use of cookies in your region. Use a banner to inform users about the use of cookies and obtain consent from users. Do not interfere with users' Do Not Track browser options.
4. Anonymize the data: Remove any information that can be linked to an individual user, such as IP address, name, email, etc., or pseudonymize information using encryption or by replacing information with a coded or random identifier. Use aggregate data that tracks groups rather than individual users.
5. Secure the data: Any data that is collected should be protected from unauthorized access through the use of security measures such as encryption, firewalls, password protection, and access control policies. Data should have a retention policy specifying its deletion after a certain period of time.

In addition to following best practices, there are also a variety of website analytics tools that are specifically focused on user privacy. Not all these options are free like Google Analytics; however, they all have protections and policies in place to maintain users' privacy.

- Fathom Analytics
    https://usefathom.com/why-fathom-analytics/privacy-focused-web-analytics
    Free trial with pricing starting at $15/month
- Matomo
    https://matomo.org/privacy/
    Free open-source software with hosting available for $26/month
- Plausible
    https://plausible.io/privacy-focused-web-analytics
    Free trial with pricing starting at €9/month
- Simple Analytics
    https://www.simpleanalytics.com/
    Free trial with pricing starting at $9/month
- Wide Angle Analytics
    https://wideangle.co/privacy-focused-web-analytics
    Free trial with pricing starting at €9.99/month

WEBSITE ANALYTICS TOOLS

There are many different website analytics tools are available that can help you to track and analyze the activity on your website, though they don't all do the same things. There are multiple different categories[18] of analytics software to consider, including:

1. Traditional: Tools that collect quantitative data, such as the number of pageviews and length of sessions. Google Analytics is the best-known example of a traditional analytics tool, though there are numerous other options, such as Matomo and Adobe Analytics.
2. Behavioral: Tools that gather qualitative data on users' behavior, such as what they do and why, through the use of surveys, heatmapping, and user interviews. Hotjar, CrazyEgg, and FullStory are examples of behavioral analytics tools.
3. Customer journey: Tools that track the user throughout their journey on your website to provide a better analysis of the overall customer experience. Woopra, Contentsquare, and Totango all provide customer journey analytics.
4. Content analytics: Tools that measure content performance and provide data on how audiences connect with your content, including what sections have the most user engagement. Chartbeat and Parse.ly are examples of content analytics tools.
5. SEO analytics: Tools that gather data on SEO metrics, like keyword performance and search traffic. SEMRush, HubSpot, and Ahrefs all provide analytical data on a website's SEO.

Each individual analytics platform will have different features and price points to consider. Some are hosted on your site by including code snippets that track data, like Google Analytics, while others come from third-party sources that can generate analytical data about multiple websites. While research has found that as much as "88 percent of libraries surveyed had implemented Google Analytics or Google Tag Manager,"[19] as of 2018, Google is not the only option for gathering analytics data. The following list contains some of the more currently popular analytics tools for website assessment.

- Adobe Analytics
    https://business.adobe.com/products/analytics/adobe-analytics.html
    Adobe Analytics is a traditional analytics tool that is part of the Adobe Experience Platform. Adobe Analytics is geared mostly toward enterprise sites. It can gather data from multiple channels and segment users, and it can use AI and machine learning to model customer behavior. You must submit a request to receive a quote for pricing.

- Ahrefs
    https://ahrefs.com/
    Ahrefs is a comprehensive SEO analytics tool that can be used to analyze customer keyword searches, as well as to audit your site's technical SEO optimization and perform competitor analysis. There is a free version with access to Site Explorer (competitor analysis) and Site Audit (SEO auditing), as well as several paid plans with additional features.
- Crazy Egg
    https://www.crazyegg.com/
    Crazy Egg provides behavioral analysis through the use of heatmaps, recordings, surveys, A/B testing, and traffic analysis. Crazy Egg offers a free 30-day trial with pricing starting at $49 per month for a standard plan up to $249 per month for an enterprise level plan.
- Google Analytics
    https://marketingplatform.google.com/about/analytics/
    Google Analytics is one of the best-known analytics tools and is freely available online. Google Analytics requires a piece of tracking code to be installed within your website code and tracks quantitative data like the number of unique visitors, page visits, bounce rate, and referring URLs.
- Hotjar
    https://www.hotjar.com/
    Hotjar provides behavioral analytics through heatmapping, surveys, session recordings, and user interviews. Hotjar can also be integrated with other traditional web analytics tools such as Google Analytics. There is a basic free version, which includes automatic data capture and heatmaps, as well as several levels of paid options with additional features.
- Kissmetrics
    https://www.kissmetrics.io/
    Kissmetrics tracks quantitative data as well as behavioral data through event tracking. Kissmetrics has plans starting at $25.99 per month, or "pay as you go" options from $0.0025 per event.
- Matomo
    https://matomo.org/
    Matomo, formerly known as Piwik, is an open-source analytics tool that has become popular with libraries as an alternative to Google Analytics. Matomo is user-privacy focused, and you retain full ownership of any data you gather. Matomo can be self-hosted for free. There is also the option to have the vendor host the software for $26 per month, which includes vendor support. However, with vendor hosting, your data will be stored in Europe rather than the location of your choosing, which can sometimes conflict with organizational policy.

- Open Web Analytics
  https://www.openwebanalytics.com/
  Open Web Analytics is another free and open-source analytics software that can be used as an alternative to Google Analytics. Open Web Analytics provides the standard quantitative metrics as well as qualitative data gathered through heatmapping, clickstream data, and tracking clicks on DOM elements. As a fully free and open-source software, help is limited to community support.

ADDITIONAL RESOURCES

- Farney, Tabatha, and Nina McHale. *Web Analytics Strategies for Information Professionals: A LITA Guide*. Chicago: ALA Neal-Schuman, 2013.
- Farney, Tabatha. *Using Digital Analytics for Smart Assessment*. Chicago: ALA Editions, 2018.
- Marek, Kate. "Using Web Analytics in the Library." *Library Technology Reports 47*, no. 5 (2011).
- Showers, Ben. *Library Analytics and Metrics: Using Data to Drive Decisions and Services*. London: Facet Publishing, 2015.

NOTES

1. Wei Fang, "Google Analytics and Library Web Sites," in *The Complete Guide to Using Google in Libraries: Instruction, Administration, and Staff Productivity, Volume 1*, ed. Carol Smallwood (Lanham: Rowman & Littlefield, 2015), 107.
2. Le Yang and Joy M. Perrin, "Tutorials on Google Analytics: How to Craft a Web Analytics Report for a Library Web Site," *Journal of Web Librarianship* 8, no. 4 (2014): 410, https://doi.org/10.1080/19322909.2014.944296.
3. Julie Arendt and Cassie Wagner, "Beyond Description: Converting Web Site Usage Statistics into Concrete Site Improvement Ideas," *Journal of Web Librarianship* 4, no. 1 (2010): 4, https://doi.org/10.1080/19322900903547414.
4. Arendt and Wagner, 6.
5. Anindita Paul and Sanda Erdelez, "Implementation and Use of Web Analytics for Academic Library Websites," *World Digital Libraries* 6, no. 2 (2013): 122, https://content.iospress.com/articles/world-digital-libraries-an-international-journal/wdl120106.
6. Wei Fang, "Using Google Analytics for Improving Library Website Content and Design: A Case Study," *Library Philosophy and Practice* 121 (2007): 13, https://digitalcommons.unl.edu/libphilprac/121.
7. Fang, 11.
8. Arendt and Wagner, 5–6.
9. Arendt and Wagner, 5.

10. Jody Condit Fagan, "The Suitability of Web Analytics Key Performance Indicators in the Academic Library Environment," *Journal of Academic Librarianship* 40, no. 1 (2014): 25, https://doi.org/10.1016/j.acalib.2013.06.005.
11. James Moore Jr., "Balancing Power with Responsibility: How Academic Libraries Balance Web Analytics and Patron Privacy," (2017): 6, https://doi.org/10.17615/d7rr-a960.
12. Denise Quintel and Robert Wilson, "Analytics and Privacy: Using Matomo in EBSCO's Discovery Service," *Information Technology and Libraries* 39, no. 3 (2020): 2–3, https://doi.org/10.6017/ital.v39i3.12219.
13. Paul and Erdelez, 118.
14. Quintel and Wilson, 6.
15. Quintel and Wilson, 5.
16. Moore, 25.
17. Google Analytics Terms of Service, https://marketingplatform.google.com/about/analytics/terms/us/.
18. "Top 12+ Web Analytics Tools to Improve Your Site and Grow Your Business," Hotjar, January 31, 2024, https://www.hotjar.com/web-analytics/tools/.
19. Quintel and Wilson, 2.

BIBLIOGRAPHY

"Google Analytics Terms of Service." Google. May 15, 2023. https://marketingplatform.google.com/about/analytics/terms/us/.

"Top 12+ Web Analytics Tools to Improve Your Site and Grow Your Business." Hotjar. January 31, 2024. https://www.hotjar.com/web-analytics/tools/.

Arendt, Julie, and Cassie Wagner. "Beyond Description: Converting Web Site Usage Statistics into Concrete Site Improvement Ideas." *Journal of Web Librarianship* 4, no. 1 (2010): 37–54. https://doi.org/10.1080/19322900903547414.

Fagan, Jody Condit. "The Suitability of Web Analytics Key Performance Indicators in the Academic Library Environment." *Journal of Academic Librarianship* 40, no. 1 (2014): 25–34. https://doi.org/10.1016/j.acalib.2013.06.005.

Fang, Wei. "Using Google Analytics for Improving Library Website Content and Design: A Case Study." *Library Philosophy and Practice* 121 (2007). https://digitalcommons.unl.edu/libphilprac/121.

Fang, Wei. "Google Analytics and Library Web Sites." In *The Complete Guide to Using Google in Libraries: Instruction, Administration, and Staff Productivity, Volume 1*, edited by Carol Smallwood, 107–20. Lanham: Rowman & Littlefield, 2015.

Moore Jr., James. "Balancing Power with Responsibility: How Academic Libraries Balance Web Analytics and Patron Privacy." (2017). https://doi.org/10.17615/d7rr-a960.

Paul, Anindita, and Sanda Erdelez. "Implementation and Use of Web Analytics for Academic Library Websites." *World Digital Libraries* 6, no. 2 (2013):

115–32. https://content.iospress.com/articles/world-digital-libraries-an
-international-journal/wdl120106.

Quintel, Denise, and Robert Wilson. "Analytics and Privacy: Using Matomo in EBSCO's Discovery Service." *Information Technology and Libraries* 39, no. 3 (2020). https://doi.org/10.6017/ital.v39i3.12219.

Yang, Le, and Joy M. Perrin. "Tutorials on Google Analytics: How to Craft a Web Analytics Report for a Library Web Site." *Journal of Web Librarianship* 8, no. 4 (2014): 404–17. https://doi.org/10.1080/19322909.2014.944296.

10

Ongoing Maintenance

Once your new website has been designed, coded, tested, and launched, it might seem like there is nothing left to do until the next big redesign project. However, work on the library website should not stop once the new site is up and running. In addition to regular assessment and incremental improvements, as discussed in chapter 9, having a website maintenance plan in place is also important to keep the new site up-to-date and fully functional well into the future. Regular maintenance and ongoing assessment can also prevent the need for additional large-scale redesign projects or make them less frequently needed.

We have all come across websites on the internet that were created years, or even decades ago, and then were seemingly abandoned or never updated.[1] Then there are the websites that were created in a more modern era and perhaps occasionally updated, but still seem to always have outdated or inaccurate information, broken links, or non-functioning features. Although these websites are plentiful, they are not typically the type of websites that visitors frequently use or come back to. Unmaintained websites can cause users to distrust the site (asking themselves, Is this information accurate? Or why doesn't the registration form work?), or even distrust the organization (If they aren't keeping the website up-to-date, what else are they neglecting?).

Failing to maintain the website you just spent months or years creating can also quickly diminish the work that was put into it. Some of the problems that can creep up on a website that is not being actively maintained include:

- Slower loading times: Not paying attention to page speed or site performance can lead to neglecting opportunities to make your website faster, such as minimizing large images or files, or reducing the amount of code being loaded on the page. The slower a website gets, the more frustrating it is for visitors to use. Many users will give up and find a website that is better functioning to use instead.

- Browser compatibility issues: Internet browsers, like Chrome and Firefox, tend to get updated with some regularity, with new versions featuring improved functionality, compliance with newer security standards, and the integration of more modern technology protocols and frameworks. If a website is not keeping up with ongoing browser and technology changes, it is more likely that users with updated browsers will begin to experience issues or even the inability to use the site.
- Frequent browser crashes: A website that is using outdated software may be more prone to crashing the browser, especially if users are visiting the site with the newest browser versions. A website that causes frequent browser crashes will quickly become very unpopular with users.
- Security vulnerabilities: Security standards are constantly changing in response to new exploits created by attackers and if the website is not updated to comply with new security standards or is not being protected by the installation of up-to-date security patches, the site can become vulnerable to malware, injections, and theft of data. These security vulnerabilities can potentially cause many issues for the site if attackers gain access and use it to install malware on users' computers or steal their personal data. These kinds of breaches can be costly both in terms of the financial cost of recovering from an attack, as well as the cost of losing the trust of your patrons.
- Errors and bugs: Easily fixed errors can be accidentally inserted into the website code during updates or site changes, but if someone is regularly monitoring the website, they can be corrected before causing any problems. However, if no one is monitoring the site, it is likely to be a user who notices them first. New versions of software will also sometimes have bugs in the code that cause issues and can be fixed with a patch or an update to a maintenance version as long as someone is regularly tracking and installing updates to the site.
- Non-functioning plugins: Many plugins for content management systems like WordPress are created by users and released to the public for community use. These custom plugins may or may not be maintained by their creators. Unmaintained plugins can lose functionality as software changes over time, or they can become exploited by cyberattackers, leaving your website more vulnerable to security issues.
- Outdated design: Website trends are sometimes around for a short time, or they can be popular for a number of years before they are replaced with new trends and design elements. If a website is not regularly updated to incorporate newer design trends, it will begin to look dated to the user over time. Regular updates to include new popular features or remove outdated design elements can keep your website looking fresh and help reduce the need for a major website redesign.

None of these problems are things you want your website visitors to have to deal with. Letting your site go unmaintained can lead to multiple and ever-increasing problems, and users may eventually lose trust in the website and possibly the organization. While regular maintenance can prevent many different issues that can become serious problems, it also greatly benefits your website, and by extension, your organization. Some of the benefits of regular website maintenance include:

- Improved security: Outdated plugins, not backing up your site, and not implementing timely security patches can leave your site vulnerable to cyberattacks and other security issues. An updated website is more secure against potential security attacks.
- Optimized functionality: Keeping the site up-to-date with new technology, including updated plugins, browser compatibility, and compressed image files, will ensure that it stays functional even when visitors are using the newest or most updated browsers or if they are using a slow internet bandwidth.
- Boost in traffic and search engine rankings: Google ranks websites that are regularly updated higher than websites that are not regularly maintained. With the right SEO, your website can appear at the top of the page of search results, rather than gradually slipping further and further down the page.
- Improved user experience: A website that is optimized for page speed, up-to-date with security and accessibility compliance, and fully functioning will provide a better user experience for the visitor. Better user experience usually translates to repeat visits and the establishment of trust with your patrons.
- Improved site performance: A website that is regularly maintained will have better performance metrics than one that has not been maintained. This includes things like improved load time, page speed, session durations, and bounce rates.
- Saving time and money: If a site has been left unmaintained for an extended period of time, it will eventually require a great deal of effort to extensively redesign and update the site. Major redesign projects can be expensive, requiring skilled staff or consultants, as well as time-consuming. Putting the time and effort into smaller amounts of regular maintenance can avoid the expense of a major redesign project down the road.

TYPES OF MAINTENANCE

There are several different types of maintenance that need to be regularly performed to keep a website in good shape. While each of these maintenance types affects different aspects of the overall website, each is important and needs to be incorporated into your regular maintenance schedule. Some of the basic types of website maintenance that need to be performed on a regular schedule include:

- Security updates: To maintain the security of your website, you will need to regularly perform security updates, including staying aware of current security issues and regularly installing security patches issued for the CMS or other software. If the CMS is hosted by the vendor, they may take care of any necessary security updates for you.
- Search engine optimization: You can ensure that your site stays optimized for SEO by regularly tracking rankings, backlinks, and website traffic. Regular monitoring of SEO can help you identify problems and fix them quickly to ensure that the website appears at the top of search results and that your visitors are able to easily find it.
- Content updates: The content on your website should be frequently updated to ensure that it stays relevant and accurate. Regularly remove or update outdated information, add new information relevant to your patrons, and keep any dynamic content, such as blog posts up-to-date. It is better to remove an unused blog from the website than to have one that hasn't been updated in months or even years.
- Backup/disaster recovery: A full backup of the website should be performed regularly in case of any catastrophic server issues or data loss. A recent full backup will ensure that the website can quickly be restored to a recent version in the event of unexpected disasters.
- Performance optimization: The website's performance should be regularly monitored via an analytics platform such as Google Analytics, so that it can be optimized for things like site speed and load time, image and file size reduction, minimizing HTTP requests, and applying caching measures. Regular performance monitoring can allow you to quickly find and remediate any potential issues before they become too large.
- User management: Regular website maintenance includes user management tasks, such as creating or deleting user accounts, resetting passwords, managing website roles and permissions, and removing any spam accounts. Some of these user management tasks, such as deleting accounts for inactive users and removing spam, are important security measures as well.
- Accessibility: The website should be regularly reviewed for accessibility compliance to ensure that it stays accessible as changes are made or new content is added to the site. For example, is alt text always being applied when new images are added? Regular accessibility checks will ensure that content creators are still following accessibility guidelines. You will also

need to keep up with any changing accessibility guidelines or requirements to ensure that the site stays compliant as legal requirements change.
- Uptime monitoring: You want your website to be available any time it is needed, and the best way to guarantee this is monitoring the site's uptime. The uptime should be as close to 100 percent as possible. You'll want to be notified ASAP if the website goes down so that it can be addressed and brought up and running again as quickly as possible. If you pay for website hosting, the vendor will monitor uptime, and there is likely to be a service level agreement (SLA) defining the percentage of uptime that the vendor is committed to providing (such as 99.99 percent).

Table 10.1 lists some of the maintenance tasks that should be done on a regular basis in order to effectively maintain your website.

WEBSITE GOVERNANCE

Ensuring regular maintenance of a website is helped immensely by developing a solid website governance plan. *Website governance* "entails the coordination of content maintenance and management of the full content life cycle from creation through revision or retirement, including measurement and evaluation through analysis of usage data, testing, and other means"[2] and requires clear processes, policies, and procedures, including delegating decision-making authority.

It is important to establish at the outset who has the authority, as well as the responsibility, to make changes, additions, deletions, and updates to the website, and who is the final decision-maker when it comes to what changes will be made. A website governance plan can use a centralized model of responsibility, where the website is managed by one person, or a distributed model, where responsibility is divided between a committee, team, or advisory group. It is recommended that there be a designated web manager "to allow for continuity in the evolution of the website."[3]

Defining Roles and Responsibilities

Well-defined roles and responsibilities establish who is responsible for what when it comes to managing website content. Some of the roles that should be established, along with their responsibilities, include the following:[4]

- Requestor: The person or persons who request new content, edits, or deletions.
- Provider: The person who provides or creates the content.
- Manager: The person who edits and manages the overall life cycle of the content.

Table 10.1   Website maintenance tasks.

Security Maintenance Tasks

- Perform regular security scans.
- Install security patches.
- Update CMS software.
- Update plugins, modules, and themes.
- Delete unnecessary plug-ins and modules.
- Update SSL certificates.
- Renew domain registration.
- Update malware and virus protection.
- Check firewall rules and .htaccess settings.
- Check access logs for compromised accounts.
- Update system passwords.
- Conduct regular security audits.

Content Maintenance Tasks

- Create and publish new content.
- Update or remove outdated information and images.
- Check for broken links and missing images.
- Check forms, pop-ups, buttons, and other interactive features.
- Check contact information for accuracy.
- Moderate any site comments or user-generated content.
- Conduct regular content audits.

Performance Maintenance Tasks

- Review error logs/check for 404 pages.
- Check for script errors.
- Check page speed/load time.
- Optimize images, minify CSS and JS files, and implement caching mechanisms.
- Review server load.
- Check for bugs and browser compatibility issues.
- Track website rankings and backlinks.
- Check mobile responsiveness.
- Review site uptime.
- Check SEO performance.
- Review and analyze site metrics.

Other Maintenance Tasks

- Create/delete user accounts.
- Review/manage user roles and permissions.
- Remove spam/bot accounts.
- Configure email accounts.
- Perform full backup of website files and database.
- Verify integrity of site backups.
- Gather feedback from users.
- Update copyright notice.
- Update privacy policy/other policies.
- Optimize database.
- Perform regular accessibility audits.
- Perform regular usability testing.

- Reviewer: The person who reviews content before publication.
- Publisher: The person who publishes the content to the web.

In some cases, one person may end up occupying more than one role in the governance of the website, especially in situations where there is only a small staff available. Regardless, it is important to establish who will be responsible for making the changes and who will be the final decision-maker. You should also consider who needs to be consulted on or informed about what changes.

In addition to defining roles and responsibilities for managing the content on the website, there should also be a person or persons designated for handling the technical aspects of the website. This includes things like:

- Who will perform software updates, site backups, annual domain registration, and performance monitoring?
- Who will gather and analyze website analytics and other data?
- Who will be responsible for search engine optimization?
- Who will conduct accessibility and security audits?
- Who will perform usability testing and recommend improvements to the site?

In a small library with limited staff, this may all be handled by a single person. Often in smaller libraries, both the content and technical aspects of website management are handled by a single person whose entire job consists of managing all aspects of the website—the web librarian. In larger libraries with a bigger staff and more division of labor, there may be a content manager tasked with managing content strategy and content creation, a web manager to write code and make website updates, an IT department to handle server updates and security, and/or a UX librarian to be responsible for usability testing and accessibility compliance.

Whether there is a single website manager or multiple people taking part in website maintenance, those responsible will need to stay up-to-date with web developments and "changes throughout the internet, including software, hardware, and other IT issues."[5]

Establishing Workflows

Once roles and responsibilities have been established, you will need to create workflows for various tasks involved in the maintenance of the website, including creating new content, updating content, and deleting content. Workflows don't necessarily need to be complicated, but they establish a procedure for making changes that ensures that everything that needs to be done gets done and that everyone who needs to be involved is included in the process. Some potential workflows designed by library UX professional and content strategist Rebecca Blakiston include:

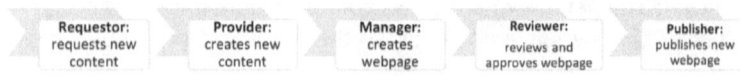

Figure 10.1 Sample workflow for creating a new webpage. Brighid M. Gonzales.[6]

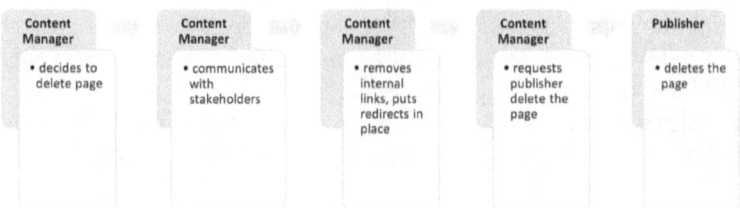

Figure 10.2 Sample workflow for deleting a webpage. Brighid M. Gonzales.[7]

Developing a Regular Maintenance Schedule

One of the best ways to ensure that everything that needs to be done gets done is to create a maintenance schedule that lays out exactly how often various tasks should occur. A regular schedule ensures that tasks are done in a timely manner and that nothing gets accidentally overlooked. There is not necessarily one designated schedule of tasks that will work for every library, and different experts will sometimes recommend different schedules for the same tasks. For instance, do you need to check comments for spam every week or every day? It depends on the number of comments your website receives and how much spam tends to target the site. Security scans and updates should be performed at least monthly; however, if an urgent security patch is released by the vendor, then it should be applied as soon as possible. Meanwhile, accessibility audits and usability testing may only need to be performed once a year, especially if there is not a person for whom it is their main job responsibility.

The important thing is to ensure that every necessary maintenance task gets added to the schedule and that each one is performed often enough that problems are not allowed to linger or build up. Table 10.2 provides an example of a schedule that includes some of the most important maintenance tasks.

Website Maintenance Tools

Conducting regular website maintenance can be a time-consuming process, especially if it's done manually and by a single person. However, there are a number of free and commercial tools that can be used to automate things like security and accessibility auditing, SEO optimization, performance and uptime monitoring, and other regular maintenance tasks. Some of the tools that can be used to assist in website maintenance include the following:

- Acunetix
    https://www.acunetix.com/
    Acunetix is a web application security scanner software that you can use to automate security scanning, find and remediate security vulnerabilities, and learn about new zero-day exploits. You will need to submit a form to request a price quote.
- Ahrefs
    https://ahrefs.com/
    Ahrefs is an online SEO tool kit that can be used to audit and optimize your website's SEO, find keywords being used by your site visitors, and analyze competitor websites. There are several paid options as well as free limited use access.
- Akismet
    https://akismet.com/
    Akismet is an automated spam filter that can filter out spam in comments, forms, and text. Akismet has various paid options for commercial use.
- Burp Suite
    https://portswigger.net/burp/communitydownload
    Burp Suite is a website security testing software that includes a "Community Edition," which can be downloaded and used at no charge.
- FileZilla
    https://filezilla-project.org/
    FileZilla is free open-source FTP (file transfer protocol) software that can be used to transfer files to and from the server and to perform website backups. FileZilla can be used with Windows, Linux, or Mac operating systems.
- Google PageSpeed Insights
    https://pagespeed.web.dev/
    PageSpeed Insights is a free online tool from Google that allows you to analyze your page speed and get recommendations for how to make your site faster.
- GTmetrix
    https://gtmetrix.com/
    GTmetrix is an online software suite that can test your website load speed by simulating website visits from different countries, browsers, and connection speeds. It can also test how fast your site loads on different devices. It is free to try, with several paid options.
- Pingdom
    https://www.pingdom.com/
    Pingdom can be used to automate website uptime and performance monitoring. Pingdom can monitor page speed, provide visitor insights, and simulate user interactions. They offer a thirty-day free trial.

Table 10.2   Example website maintenance schedule.

Schedule	Maintenance Tasks
Weekly	• Update plugins. • Check for broken links. • Check comments/remove spam comments. • Install software updates. • Back up website.
Monthly	• Database maintenance. • Test site speed. • Check security scans/perform security updates. • Delete unused plugins. • Monitor site performance/analytics. • Check for 404 errors.
Quarterly	• Perform an SEO audit. • Update graphics/reduce image sizes. • Update page metadata. • Check for mobile optimization. • Test forms and interactive components. • Perform a content audit.
Annually	• Renew domain registration. • Renew SSL certificate. • Test browser compatibility. • Update header/footer information (contact info, terms of service, privacy policy, copyright info, etc.). • Review current website design trends. • Conduct an accessibility audit. • Conduct a security audit. • Conduct usability testing.

- Sucuri

    https://sucuri.net/

    Sucuri is a website security tool with various paid plan options that can be used for malware detection, integrity monitoring, and server hardening.
- Siteimprove

    https://www.siteimprove.com/

    Siteimprove is an online marketing performance platform that can be used to optimize SEO through behavioral insights, funnel comparison, user journeys, and key metrics. It can also be used to automate accessibility, link, and spell checks. You will need to submit a form to get a price quote.

- WinSCP
    https://winscp.net/eng/index.php
    WinSCP is another free file transfer software that can be used with Windows. WinSCP can use multiple protocols including FTP, FTPS, SCP, SFTP, WebDAV, and Amazon S3.

ADDITIONAL RESOURCES

- Blokdyk, Gerardus. *Website Management: A Clear and Concise Reference*. La Vergne: Emereo Publishing, 2018.
- Buchanan, Sherry. "A Toolkit to Effectively Manage Your Website: Practical Advice for Content Strategy." *Weave: Journal of Library User Experience* 1, no. 6 (2017). https://doi.org/10.3998/weave.12535642.0001.604.
- Diffily, Shane. *The Website Manager's Handbook*. Morrisville, NC: Lulu, 2006.
- Intal, Benjamin. *WordPress Maintenance: Keeping Your Website Safe and Efficient*. Freiburg: Smashing Magazine, 2015.
- "Website Maintenance Checklist." Process Street. Accessed May 9, 2024. https://www.process.st/templates/website-maintenance-checklist/.

NOTES

1. Original Space Jam website, https://www.spacejam.com/1996/.
2. Courtney McDonald and Heidi Burkhardt, "Web Content Strategy in Academic Libraries: Methods and Maturity," *portal: Libraries and the Academy* 22, no. 4 (2022): 1010, https://doi.org/10.1353/pla.2022.0050.
3. Jo Golding, Alison Carter, and Cathie Koina, "Library Website Management Guidelines: What You Need to Know," *Australian Library Journal* 49, no. 1 (2000): 55, https://doi.org/10.1080/00049670.2000.10755907.
4. Rebecca Blakiston, "Content Strategy for Library Websites," February 26, 2015, Slide 43, https://www.slideshare.net/steadfastlibrarian/content-strategy-for-library-websites.
5. Golding, Carter, and Koina, 56.
6. Blakiston, slide 49.
7. Blakiston, slide 50.

BIBLIOGRAPHY

Blakiston, Rebecca. "Content Strategy for Library Websites." February 26, 2015. https://www.slideshare.net/steadfastlibrarian/content-strategy-for-library-websites.

Golding, Jo, Alison Carter, and Cathie Koina. "Library Website Management Guidelines: What You Need to Know." *The Australian Library Journal* 49, no. 1 (2000): 51–56. https://doi.org/10.1080/00049670.2000.10755907.

McDonald, Courtney, and Heidi Burkhardt. "Web Content Strategy in Academic Libraries: Methods and Maturity." *portal: Libraries and the Academy* 22, no. 4 (2022): 995–1033. https://doi.org/10.1353/pla.2022.0050.

Index

abbreviations. *See* acronyms
access control. *See* permissions
accessibility, 5, 8, 12, 23, 26, 35, 42, 50, 59-61, 71-73, 78, 93-96, 100-108, 143-44;
  audit of, 97, 146, 149, 150;
  errors, 61, 97-99, 107;
  evaluation of, 96, 106-108;
  principles of, 96-97;
  tools, 107-108
acronyms, 9, 25, 70
ADA. *See* Americans with Disabilities Act
AI. *See* artificial intelligence
alt text, 4-6, 42, 58, 98-99, 105, 144
American Library Association:
  code of ethics, 121, 133;
  library privacy, 53, 112, 124;
  privacy tool kit, 122, 124
Americans with Disabilities Act:
  compliance, 40, 42, 59-60, 93, 95, 108, 128
analytics, 42, 54, 59-61, 70, 79, 89-90, 127-38;
  metrics, 51, 54, 61, 129-32, 138, 143, 146;
  privacy, ix, 53, 111-12, 121-24, 133-35;
  tools, 61, 128-29, 133, 135-38
animations, 15-16
anti-virus software, 5, 117, 146
APIs. *See* application programming interface

application programming interface, 38-39, 116
Arango, Jorge, 63, 66
artificial intelligence, 17
assessment, 42-43, 54-55, 60, 112, 127-28, 136, 141.
  See also analytics
assistive technology, 94-97, 100-104, 107
attitudinal research, 79, 82
audio/video. *See* multimedia
authentication, 5, 36-37, 42, 112-118

Bailie, Rahel, 58
behavioral research, 79, 137
best practices, 3-6, 8-10, 23-24, 47, 51-52, 72-73, 80-81, 84, 95, 115-18, 120, 123, 134-35
BiblioCommons, 46
BiblioWeb, 39, 46
Black, Elizabeth, 40
Blakiston, Rebecca, 17, 61, 90, 148
Bootstrap, 5, 15, 42
Brown, Dan, 65
browser compatibility, 41, 131, 142-43, 146, 150
buttons, 4, 7, 15-16, 27, 73, 86, 105, 146

captions, 15, 98, 103, 105-106
card sorting, 67, 70, 74, 79, 83-84, 90, 128
carousels, 26, 72
chat, 22, 28, 54, 100, 106

153

chunking, 4, 9, 52, 60, 67
CIA triad, 121
CMS. *See* content management systems
cognitive load, 7, 64
color:
   and accessibility, 98, 103, 105;
   color palette, 1, 2, 4-5, 8, 12-15, 17, 27-28, 105;
   color wheel, 12, 14;
   contrast, 4, 5, 7, 98, 103
consistency, 2, 4-5, 7-9, 14, 24, 35-36, 52, 59-60, 65, 70, 72, 99, 105
contact information, 4, 8, 21-22, 24-25, 59, 69, 72, 84, 106, 123, 146, 150
content audit, 49-51, 58-61, 150;
   rubric, 58;
   tools, 60-61
content inventory, 49-51, 55-58, 67
content lifecycle, 51
content management systems, 35-46, 51, 58, 111, 142, 144, 146;
   architecture, 37-39;
   requirements, 40
content strategist, 51, 53, 148
content strategy, 49-61, 147, 151
cookies, 113, 130, 133-35
costs, 36, 38, 41, 142-43
css, 15, 35, 40, 97, 105, 146
customer support, 42-44, 46

data model. *See* prototypes
data privacy, 121, 123, 133-34;
   audit, 122-23;
   policy, 123-24, 111-12
decision-making, 64-65
design trends, 6, 15-17
Detzi, Chris, 49
digital asset management, 36-37, 46
Drupal, 38-39, 43, 44-45, 47

encryption, 5, 116, 121-22, 135
error messages, 7, 103, 106, 113

extensions, 36, 41-42

file transfer protocol, 149, 151
firewalls, 5, 36, 42, 112, 116-17, 135, 146
first click testing, 68, 79, 86-87, 79, 90, 128
focus groups, 54, 59, 67, 79, 82-83, 128-29
fonts, 2, 5, 8-9, 11, 15, 36, 105;
   web safe, 4, 11, 13.
   See also typography
footer, 24, 35-36, 69, 72-73, 150
forms, 15, 25, 40, 55, 59, 97, 98, 103, 106, 112-13, 116-17, 121, 131, 146, 150;
   accessibility of, 98
FTP. *See* file transfer protocol

GDPR. *See* general data protection regulation
general data protection regulation, 133-134
golden ratio, 2
Google Analytics, 54, 60-61, 70, 90, 128, 131, 133, 135-38, 144
governance, 49, 51, 55, 145-48
gradients, 16
grid, 1-3, 5, 17, 72

Halvorson, Kristina, 53, 16
header, 4, 16, 24, 35-36, 71, 150
headings, 2, 4-7, 9-11, 15, 52, 58, 60, 66, 97, 99, 105
html, 35, 40, 42, 97, 100-101, 105, 113, 116

icons, 5-7, 15, 23, 27-28, 72-73, 99, 105
illustrations, 10, 16
images, 2, 4, 15-16, 23, 55, 105, 128, 143-44, 150;
   accessibility of, 98;
   hero image, 27

information architecture, 63-66, 74-76, 86;
  components of, 66;
  design of, 67-68;
  principles of, 65-66;
  tools, 74
interactivity, 15-17, 53, 97, 99-100, 146, 150

jargon, 9, 24-25, 67, 72, 77, 105, 123
Joomla!, 38-39, 43-45
journey map, 55

keyboard navigation, 71, 98-100, 105
Krug, Steve, 17, 88, 90
Kupersmith, John, 70

labels, 4, 15, 24, 63-64, 66-68, 72, 77, 83-86, 98-99, 101, 105-106. *See also* terminology
LAMP stack, 37, 41
Land, Paula, 58
layout, 1-2, 5-7, 15, 17, 35-36, 41, 45, 85, 105
legal requirements, 10, 23, 51, 93-94, 124, 134-35
Leibtag, Ahava, 50
LibGuides, 37, 39, 43, 46-47
Library Information Systems Security Assessment Model, 112
links, 4, 7, 9, 15, 22, 24, 26-27, 40, 50-51, 58-60, 68, 71-72, 86, 96, 99, 105, 132, 141, 146, 150;
  accessibility of, 86, 99;
  quick links, 22, 24
lists, 9, 52, 60, 100
logos, 7, 11, 28, 69, 103, 105

maintenance, 35, 50-51, 141-51;
  tasks, 143-46, 150;
  tools, 148-151
malware, 36, 113-14, 117, 121, 142, 146, 150;
  anti-malware, 5, 117
MAMP stack, 37

Matomo, 128, 133, 135-37
mental models, 64, 83
menu. *See* navigation
metrics. *See* analytics
migration, 51
mobile-friendly, 4, 6, 8, 16, 23, 26, 41-42, 60, 69, 71-73, 94, 104-105, 128, 131, 133, 146, 150
modules, 45, 146
Morville, Peter, 63, 66, 75, 78
multimedia, 8, 15, 26, 42, 50, 55, 93, 96, 98, 103, 106

navigation, 4, 7, 15, 24, 26-27, 35-36, 41, 63-73, 77, 84-86, 99, 105, 132;
  breadcrumbs, 26, 65-66, 69, 71, 73, 105;
  design of, 67-69;
  dropdown, 7, 27, 71;
  hamburger menu, 7, 28, 69, 71, 73;
  hierarchy, 26-27, 55, 60;
  mobile, 73;
  patterns, 69-72;
  tools, 74
needs assessment, 49, 51-54, 59
Nielsen, Jakob, 6, 9, 77, 88
Nielsen Norman, 50, 91

Omeka, 46
Open-source, 36, 41-43, 45-46, 57, 135, 137-38, 149

page load speed, 4-6, 8, 11, 16, 23, 26, 41, 61, 128, 132, 141, 143-44, 146, 149
passwords, 5, 113-14, 116-19, 135
permissions, 36, 40, 43, 111, 117, 122, 135, 144, 146
personalization, 6, 15, 17, 22, 40, 123
plain language, 9-10, 25, 52, 60, 70, 72, 97, 104, 123
plugins, 5, 36, 41-42, 45, 111, 116-17, 142-43, 146, 150
pop-ups, 8, 28, 114, 146

preference testing, 87
prototypes, 67-68, 74, 85-87

qualitative audit. *See* content audit
qualitative research, 79, 82, 85, 87, 90, 128-29, 132, 137-38
quantitative audit. *See* content inventory

readability, 4, 7, 10-11, 52, 59-60, 105
Rehabilitation Act of 1973 section 508, 93, 95, 108, 128
responsive design, 2, 4-5, 23, 35, 41-42, 53, 71, 73
rich internet applications, 97
Rosenfeld, Louis, 63, 66, 75
RSS feeds, 40

SaaS, 39, 46
scalability, 5, 41-42, 73
scrolling, 16, 26, 71
search, 4, 7, 22, 24, 27, 41, 54, 59, 61, 63, 66, 69-70, 100, 132
search bar. *See* search
search box. *See* search
search engine optimization, 6, 17, 35-36, 41-42, 51, 58, 61, 128, 136-37, 143-44, 146, 148-151
security, 5, 23, 25, 36, 38, 42-44, 103, 111-122, 124, 127-28, 135, 142-44, 146-150;
    attacks, 112-16;
    audit, 119-21;
    benchmarks, 120;
    tools, 120-21, 148
SEO. *See* search engine optimization
server hardening, 117, 150
service level agreement, 145
simplicity, 5, 7, 10, 17, 27-28, 36, 52, 72, 103
social media, 6-7, 22, 72, 124, 130, 134

Solomon, Laura, 21, 29
Springshare. *See* LibGuides
ssl certification, 5, 8, 36, 42, 115-17, 120, 146, 150
standards, 6-7, 51, 53, 58, 64, 95-96, 100, 142
style guide, 8, 14-15, 17, 51-52
surveys, 53-54, 59, 67, 79-81, 89-90, 128-29, 136-37

tables, 9, 15, 40, 97
taxonomy, 51, 100.
    See also terminology
terminology, 4, 9, 15, 24-25, 52, 54, 60, 66-67, 70, 72, 77, 83, 88, 123
templates, 36, 38, 40-42, 45-46
themes, 42, 45, 146
three-click rule, 26
tone, 10, 12, 15, 51-52, 60
tree testing, 68, 74, 79, 84-85, 79, 90
typography, 1, 8, 10-11, 15-17.
    See also fonts

universal design, 93, 101-106, 108-109;
    principles of, 103-104.
    See also user-centered design
uptime, 145-46, 148, 150
usability, 6, 8, 10, 12, 15, 17, 41, 59-60, 63, 71-72, 77-78, 80, 83, 87-88, 102, 104, 127-28
usability testing, 6, 17, 24, 59, 68, 70, 74, 77-90, 107, 128, 146-48, 150
user control, 8, 26, 66, 106
user experience, 6, 15, 17, 25, 53, 55, 63-65, 75, 77-78, 90, 143;
    facets of, 78;
    honeycomb, 78;
    tools, 88-90
user interviews, 53-54, 59, 79, 81-82, 89-90, 128-29, 136-37
user journey, 54-55, 136

user persona, 54–55, 67, 104
user privacy. *See* data privacy
user research, 51–55, 67, 78–79;
   methods, 54, 79–89;
   user testing, 6, 59, 68, 79–80, 82,
      85, 88–90, 106–107, 128
user-centered design, 3, 17, 77.
   See also universal design

Vaughan, Jason, 121, 124
viruses, 5, 117, 146
visual hierarchy, 2, 4, 12
vocabulary. *See* terminology

W3C, 40, 95–97, 107–109
WAI-ARIA, 97, 99–101, 108
WAMP stack, 37

WCAG. *See* Web Content
   Accessibility Guidelines
Web Content Accessibility
   Guidelines, 59–61, 95–100,
   106–109, 128
web conventions, 6–7, 60, 64, 78,
   103, 105
web hosting, 5, 36, 39, 41, 46, 111,
   115, 117, 144–45
white space, 2, 5, 7, 9, 17, 27, 52
widgets, 25, 55, 100
wireframes. *See* prototypes
WordPress, 35, 38–39, 43–45, 47,
   111, 117, 142, 151
workflows, 36, 51, 147–49
writing for the web, 8–9, 17, 52, 105
WYSIWYG, 35, 42

About the Author

Brighid M. Gonzales has been a library technologist for ten years, starting as the systems and web services librarian at Our Lady of the Lake University in San Antonio, Texas, in 2014. She currently works as the systems librarian at the University of Memphis. Brighid is the author of the 2020 Rowman & Littlefield title *Systems Librarianship: A Practical Guide for Librarians*, and she has published multiple articles and book chapters on website design, usability, and programming, along with other library technology topics. She served for four years on the editorial committee of the *Code4Lib Journal* and has been a member of the *Weave: Journal of Library User Experience* editorial board since 2023.

www.ingramcontent.com/pod-product-compliance
Lightning Source LLC
Chambersburg PA
CBHW032005220426
43664CB00005B/145